P9-ELR-430

CHICAGOLAND GHOSTS

Thunder Bay Press

CHICAGOLAND GHOSTS

Dylan Clearfield

Published by Thunder Bay Press
Designed and typeset by Maureen MacLaughlin-Morris
Publisher: Sam Speigel
Cover design by Lynda A. Bass
Cover layout by Adventures with Nature, East Lansing, MI
Printed by Dickinson Press, Grand Rapids, MI
Illustrations by Patrick Reed

Copyright © 1997 Gary Stempien
All rights reserved

ISBN: 1-882376-41-2

No part of this book may be used or reproduced in any form
without written permission from the publishers, except in the
case of brief quotations embodied in critical reviews and ar-
ticles.

Printed in the United States of America

97 98 99 2000   1 2 3 4 5 6 7 8 9

ACKNOWLEDGEMENTS

Thanks to psychic investigators Richard Crowe and Dale Kaczmarek for keeping so many ghost stories alive by their retelling of them. A special thanks to my cousin AnnaMae Olichwier whose timely long distance research allowed me to rest this book in peace. A very special thanks to Peter Neff for his years of patient proofreading and encouragement.

To my parents who are together again as always.

TABLE OF CONTENTS

TABLE OF CONTENTS

TABLE OF CONTENTS

INTRODUCTION

Chicagoland is the home of many ghosts, ghouls and specters. The term 'Chicagoland' refers to an area that encompasses both the City of Chicago and the surrounding suburbs or approximately a one-hundred-mile square region —a large expanse over which ghosts can roam.

People from outlying regions of the country sometimes have difficulty understanding the concept of Chicagoland. Just as they are nonplussed by the uniquely Chicagoland salutation which arises at election time: "Vote early and vote often." This, of course, refers to Chicago's long history of vote fraud.

Not only were living persons advised to "Vote early and vote often," but so were the dead. The lists of registered voters in Chicago is filled with names taken from tombstones. John F. Kennedy may have been the only United States president who owed his election to ghosts. It is a commonly held belief that he would not have won the 1960 election without the votes from Cook County, Illinois—Chicagoland—which gave him the margin of victory. And many of these voters were of the ghostly variety.

It's important to get a feel for the culture of Chicagoland to get a real feel for the type of ghosts you'll be meeting. Just because the people we'll be reading about have passed on doesn't mean they've changed habits or ethnicity. Ethnic background is very important in Chicagoland, even if a person has moved to the suburbs. Ghosts do not forget their roots. Most of Chicago's ghosts have distinct ethnic backgrounds— primarily Polish, Irish, and Italian—and often haunt their old neighborhood locations such as churches, taverns, and restaurants. And, of course, there are also many gangster ghosts in Chicago.

The journey we're about to embark upon will take us to many diverse haunted sites, ranging from the location of the St. Valentine's Day massacre to the most commonplace of restaurants. I have visited almost all of the sites and have experienced unusual ghostly phenomena in many of them. Most of the haunted sites are public locations, accessible to everyone. I will tell you how to get to these haunted sites and advise you on which it would be best to avoid.

None of the stories are fictionalized; these are true ghostly accounts. I have lived in Chicagoland for more than thirty years and have gleaned this ghostly information by word of mouth and through local common knowledge.

Chicagoland is a vast area and has a large and varied ghostly population. Fortunately, many of the locations are open to the public and are quite active paranormally-speaking. Directions are supplied to many of these spots. Now it's up to you. If you get a chance to visit the Chicago area, don't forget to introduce yourself to one or more of the many available ghosts. They're there, just waiting to say *boo*!

GANGSTERLAND
SHADES OF DILLINGER & CAPONE

John Dillinger

The movie, *Manhattan Melodrama*, had been exciting, blazing with shootouts with the cops. Of course, the ending probably didn't appeal to one of its most celebrated viewers, John Herbert Dillinger, because the criminal in the movie was killed in the end. For someone like John Dillinger, *Manhattan Melodrama* must have seemed like light entertainment. After all, he'd been through many real life shootouts with the cops and had engineered three jail breaks during his days as top man on the FBI's Most Wanted list.

A person would have to wonder how much of the movie his date, Anna Sage—real name Ana Cumpanas—had seen, considering the treachery she was about to perform. Her thoughts were probably filled with the idea of the reward money she would receive for setting up Dillinger and the assistance that the FBI would give her with quashing deportation proceedings that were then pending against her. Earlier that evening, Anna had telephoned the FBI and informed them where she and Dillinger would be that night.

As the movie let out, Anna, wearing all red so as to be recognized by the FBI agents, walked on Dillinger's right, while on his left was another female friend, Polly Hamilton. In the doorway of the Biograph Theatre stood FBI agent Melvin Purvis. When Dillinger went by, Purvis lit up his cigar to signal the other FBI men to close in.

Dillinger and the two women started away from the theater. Suddenly, a group of five FBI agents sprang in front of them. Yanking a gun from his right pant's pocket, Dillinger made a break toward the alley on his left. Five shots rang out from the guns of the FBI men. Three bullets struck John Dillinger and threw him face down into the alley from the force of the discharges. It was 10:30 p.m., July 22, 1934. Dillinger's body was taken to nearby Alexian Brothers Hospital. He was pronounced officially dead at 10:50 p.m., having made his last escape.

The suddenness of the violent and bloody scene on that sultry Sunday night in July must have left its mark in the very atmosphere. To this day witnesses claim to see a silhouette of a stumbling figure in the alley alongside the Biograph Theatre, slumping and falling, only to disappear. Is this John Dillinger reenacting the last moments of his life on the mortal plane? Or is it someone else?

John Dillinger was a cunning individual. He was used to outsmarting and evading law enforcement officials. Even when he had been apprehended he had always managed to escape. Always. Like when he was incarcerated at the Crown Point facility which was lauded by the officials as 'escape proof.' Having visited the location myself, I can attest to its formidable nature.

The facility was crammed with row upon row of tiny cells and the hallways were so narrow that two people couldn't walk down them side-by-side. The moment a person was admitted to Crown Point he faced maximum security, being led after processing into a downward-sloping and darkened hallway. If a prisoner tried to make a break for it at this point he would most likely crack his skull on the sloping ceiling which was designed for just that purpose.

It is from this maximum security facility that John Dillinger escaped. According to Dillinger, he managed this feat by whittling an imitation handgun from a piece of wood; according to others, he escaped by gaining access to a supply of guns that had been smuggled in for his use.

Would a man as adept at getting out of harrowing situations be so easily taken in as he'd appeared to be on that fateful July night outside the Biograph Theatre? Would he not have observed that Anna Sage had been in frequent contact with the FBI over the preceding couple of days? Would he not have immediately noticed the dangerous situation he faced the moment he stepped out of the Biograph Theatre? He walked right past Melvin Purvis, one of the FBI's leading figures, before reaching the sidewalk. Would not Dillinger have recognized him and realized that an ambush was awaiting him? He had been in, and had escaped from, similar situations dozens of times before by being able to act instantly.

Could it be that John Dillinger knew that he'd been marked for assassination on that July night? Could it be that he sent someone who looked like him to the theater in his place and that the two women in the imposter's company played along? Could it be that the man who was gunned down in the alley outside the Biograph Theatre wasn't John Dillinger at all? Is the ghost who appears to this day in that alley the shade of a person tragically killed by mistake who continues to relive the horror? Is this ghostly figure trying to set the record straight about his true identity?

Is this mere speculation? Take into account that John Dillinger had blue eyes and that the corpse taken from the alley that night had brown eyes. Take into account that the corpse in the morgue said to be Dillinger's was actually inches shorter than Dillinger. Take into account that the man who had been shot outside the Biograph had different fingerprints than Dillinger's and that he suffered from a rheumatic heart condition, which Dillinger did not. In fact, it's quite clear that John Dillinger did NOT die in that dark alley that July night. The evidence is very strong that it was a small-time hoodlum named James Lawrence who was killed for John Dillinger and is the one who haunts the alley by proxy as well.

Didn't the FBI know that the man they had shot wasn't John Dillinger? Of course they did. Why the cover up then? Two reasons come to mind. One was that the FBI men in charge of the Chicago operation wanted to protect themselves—from the wrath of J. Edgar Hoover who had told them to get Dillinger this time . . . or else.

An alternate explanation is that Dillinger had paid off the FBI and had fled the country. Of these two, the second reason seems more likely. Why? Because the autopsy of the man who was killed in Dillinger's place wasn't released until three decades later—after those involved in the coverup had died. It seems that James Lawrence has good reason to still be haunting the alley outside the Biograph Theatre. How else would anyone ever know who had really been murdered there?

This doesn't leave John Dillinger without a ghost, however. We just have to return to the Crown Point facility in search of it. The jail here has long since been shut down but there have been many strange occurrences here since the closing. A ghostly figure has been seen in the cell that Dillinger occupied while incarcerated there. Odd noises can be heard and have been recorded, coming from all areas of this cavernous facility, especially arising from the dispensary which was more like a torture chamber than a place to provide medical help.

In any event, what is known for sure is that someone was killed in the alley outside the Biograph Theatre on July 22, 1934, and that the ghost of this person regularly appears there. It is also known that a ghostly figure appears often in John Dillinger's old cell at Crown Point. Even in death, John Dillinger continues to evade and mystify.

As of this writing, the Biograph Theatre is still standing in Chicago and is still operating as a movie house. In fact, the seat where 'John Dillinger' sat on July 22, 1934, is specially reserved for him and marked as such. Anyone can visit the Biograph Theatre. It is located on the north side of Chicago and is most easily accessible from Lake Shore Drive by taking the Belmont Street exit. Follow Belmont to Lincoln, turn right and proceed until you see the Biograph on your right.

The Crown Point facility has been closed. There has been talk of either renovating it or tearing it down. I'm not sure at this time what the decision was. At any rate, this location is not open to the public.

Al Capone

John Dillinger was only visiting Chicago when he was supposedly gunned down. It wasn't his base of operations. Chicago was Al Capone's town. At least, it became his after St. Valentine's Day 1929.

Up until that day Al had had all kinds of trouble with rival gangs trying to muscle in on his territory—Chicagoland. First there was Hymie Weiss, who Al had bumped off. Then there was Dion O'Banion, who Al also had bumped off. And now there was Bugs Moran, who Al was planning to have bumped off.

It was the early morning of St. Valentine's Day 1929. The snow had started falling the night before and was still coming down heavily. In the SMC Cartage Garage at 2122 North Clark Street, seven members of the Bugs Moran gang were gathered expecting to receive a hijacked shipment of booze. Bugs was on his way there to finalize the transaction.

But seconds before Bugs was to enter the garage he noticed a police wagon heading in that direction. Being an astute gangster, Bugs thought it might be more prudent to duck into a nearby coffee shop instead of proceeding to the garage. It was a decision that saved his life—at least for the time being. The police wagon pulled up to the garage and a group of men jumped out, two of them wearing police uniforms and carrying tommyguns. The others in the group were carrying valises with more guns. It was an Al Capone hit squad.

Capone's men burst into the garage and, despite the protestations of those inside—including a mechanic and a dentist who liked hanging around gangsters—lined them all up against the brick wall. After a deadly moment of silence, the two men in police uniforms took their places behind the lined-up men and opened fire, spraying them with hundreds of rounds of bullets. The victims dropped like straw scarecrows. They were then finished off by shotgun blasts to the head or back, using weapons taken from the valises. Six of the men died instantly. One of them, Frank Gusenberg, miraculously lived long enough to be taken to the hospital where his only statement was, "Coppers did it," before finally succumbing.

At the time of the slayings, Al Capone was conducting a meeting with newspaper reporters beside his Palm Island, Florida pool. He was never officially implicated in the St. Valentine's Day killings. But Bugs knew better, telling reporters as he was hastily departing the city, never to darken Chicagoland again, "Only Capone kills like that." To which Al responded, "They don't call him Bugs for nothing."

So, Al finally had Chicago all to himself. But shortly thereafter the IRS got hold of Al for not reporting his income taxes. He spent three years of his sentence in Alcatraz and then lived out the rest of his few remaining days on his Palm Island, Florida estate a wealthy . . . and haunted man.

Al might have succeeded in killing off all of his enemies but he couldn't fend off the ghost of one of them. The spirit of James Clark, who was Bugs Moran's brother-in-law and one of the St. Valentines's Day massacre victims, hounded Al to his grave. Many times Al was sent scurrying in terror from this relentless ghost. His bodyguards and servants more than once heard him pleading with the specter to leave him in peace. But it didn't. It continued its haunting of Al Capone until he died on January 25, 1947. Capone is buried in Mount Carmel Cemetery in Chicago.

Those who like to debunk ghosts point out that during Al's last years his mind had deteriorated from a disease he'd acquired in his youth. His illness coupled with guilt, they say, caused him to hallucinate this tormenting ghost. However, they fail to explain why just this solitary spirit would come back to haunt Al when he was responsible for the deaths of approximately five hundred people. Surely if this ghost had been conjured up by guilt it would have had a legion of spirits at its side. Maybe it was the relentless haunting of this ghost that finally drove Al mad, not his disease. It is significant that in 1931, sixteen years before his death, Capone contacted a

Al Capone's final 'resting' place. (Author's photo)

psychic named Alice Britt to help rid himself of the ghost of James Clark.

While the garage where the killings took place has long since been torn down—in an effort to clean up the city's gangster image—the spot where it used to stand is the site of many spectral phenomena. All that remains is an empty patch of thickly sodded ground between two buildings. But people who have walked their dogs past this spot can verify that something unseen still remains. Animals shy away from this stretch of ground and dogs often bristle and bark with fear.

The sound of moaning has also been heard coming from this location of bloodletting. Just as Al Capone could not escape one of his victims, neither could the City of Chicago escape its violent past by tearing down the physical reminder of it. The spirits remain and will do so for as long as they wish.

The location of the former garage on Clark Street is not too far from the Biograph Theatre and is easily accessible. It is most easily reached by once again taking Lake Shore Drive to the Belmont Street exit. Follow Belmont Street directly to Clark Street and turn right. Look for where 2122 Clark Street used to be and you've found the site of the infamous garage. Be sure to listen very carefully when you walk or drive by.

SHADY LAWYERS?

Clarence Darrow

Another Chicagoan with a ghostly story is Clarence Darrow, famed attorney. He was most well-known for his defense of the teacher who tried to instruct his high school students in the theory of evolution in what has come to be known as the Scopes Monkey Trial. Mr. Darrow also defended the thrill killers, Leopold and Loeb, getting them off with life imprisonment when nothing less than execution seemed just.

Clarence Darrow was an avowed atheist who claimed that he would come back from the dead on the anniversary of his death, March 13. And he would come back at the site where his cremated ashes had been dispersed. Apparently he has. Or his ghost has anyway.

When Darrow died his ashes were strewn from a bridge since dedicated to him—into the waters of the lagoon behind the Museum of Science and Industry in Chicago. When it was first constructed in the 1890s for the Columbian Exposition, the famous museum was accessed by water, hence the lagoon in the back. Much like in the city of Venice, people were taken by boat to the steps of the museum. Recently, a strange shadowy figure has been seen on the bridge at night by the lagoon. Observed by watchmen and custodians, the specter is a fleeting figure and is thought to belong to Clarence Darrow because it is near the site where his cremated ashes were spread. Sightings have been few and have occurred long after the fact of Darrow's death. This may be accounted for, however, because this location is off limits to the public and in a very secluded area.

Maybe the spirit by the lagoon really does belong to Clarence Darrow. If so, perhaps he's come back to plead his case for the afterlife. If anyone could make this argument it would be Darrow.

HISTORICAL HAUNTS

Screaming Rocks

Not too far outside of Chicago is Starved Rock Illinois State Park. It is reached by taking Route 80 west and then following the prominent signs. A trip here is a refreshing change for a ghosthunter from poking about crumbling deserted mansions and wandering through overgrown graveyards. At this site you can enjoy scenic beauty while seeking out apparitions in the wild.

In the early 1700s this area was occupied by the Illinois, Potawatomi, and Kickapoo tribes. They all belonged to the Algonquin language-speaking group and specifically to the Calumet clan. But this did not prevent them from hating one another. Any encroachment on another's territory was met with violent reaction.

In 1704 a war broke out that pitted the Kickapoo and Patowatomi against the Illinois. The chase led to an area in what is now Starved Rock State Park where the remaining members of the Illinois sought refuge high atop a gigantic outcrop of rock. This great rock stood by itself and had a steep drop on three sides. The fourth side faced the Illinois River hundreds of feet below. The Illinois People were trapped.

Once the Potawatomi and Kickapoo had cornered the Illinois on the outcropping all they had to do was wait. The only escape was to jump into the river which was almost certain death, although it was a route that a number of the Illinois took. Prisoners were not taken; if a person surrendered he was killed. Days and weeks passed. The few remaining Illinois slowly died of starvation. The rock to which they'd fled came to be known as Starvation Rock and the state park in turn took its name from it.

The Illinois were almost driven into extinction at Starvation Rock. However, some of them did escape, miraculously surviving the plunge into the Illinois River. Those who didn't survive the leap have apparently left their death cries in the air. Many people who have visited this site —looking for scenery not ghosts—have reported hearing shrieks coming from the top of Starvation Rock. There have also been reports of the sound of war whoops and tom-toms.

For many Illinois this last battle is still being fought and those who took refuge on Starvation Rock are still huddled there. Their plight is memorialized on a plaque in the Park which is more recognition than most Native Americans have gotten.

Fort Dearborn

Before Chicago was a city or even a village there existed Fort Dearborn. Fort Dearborn was built in 1803 by the order of Secretary of War Henry Dearborn at a narrow bend in what is now called the Chicago River. It was initially constructed as a stockade and blockhouse to fend off Indian attack which was prevalent in this then undeveloped area.

After being evacuated in 1812, Fort Dearborn was burned to the ground only to be rebuilt in 1816. Prior to the abandonment of the fort, the garrison which had manned it was massacred by Potawatomi Indians, the same Indian clan that was involved with the massacre of the Illinois tribe at Starved Rock.

The ghosts of this massacred army garrison still march the battlements of the long since demolished Fort Dearborn. Today they are seen patrolling Michigan Avenue Bridge in downtown Chicago. The Michigan Avenue Bridge was built over the site of the former Fort Dearborn and there is a plaque at the south end of the bridge in commemoration. It's a site eminently accessible by foot or car and can even be kept under observation from a park bench if a ghost hunter were so inclined.

Many sightings have been made of this phantom troop of soldiers in Revolutionary War uniforms as they continue to serve their country by manning their outpost in the hostile wilderness. Of course, Michigan Avenue today is one of the busiest streets in the world and the Michigan Avenue Bridge is one of the most widely used in the city of Chicago. Ghosts do not always or necessarily have to appear in dark secluded places. They can appear right before your eyes in the middle of a streetful of traffic and people. You may even have seen or heard a ghost and not known it. Ghosts are everywhere, waiting to be noticed.

DINING & DRINKING
WITH GHOSTS

Country House

If you take the Kingery Road exit south off Highway 55 out of Chicago you will pass through the quaint wealthy suburbs of Oak Brook and Hinsdale. At 55th Street, make a right turn and head west. Ahead of you lies the tiny village of Clarendon Hills where you've made dinner reservations at a restaurant called the 'Country House.' The restaurant is about a mile ahead on the left and you must be careful not to miss its hard-to-find parking lot. It is the only dining place in the entire residential area, but its rustic wood decor allows it to blend in almost imperceptibly with the neighborhood.

Most people who dine here probably don't know the restaurant is haunted. Most people don't venture up the long flight of stairs that's just off the kitchen because they're in an inaccessible area. I'm one of those people who did venture up those off-limit stairs one evening. Aware of the stories about ghosts and hauntings, I decided to sneak away from my dinner table to locate the source of the spectral mischief. After finding only dead ends in a poorly-marked washroom and a frantically busy kitchen area, I finally located a door that opened onto an oddly-placed flight of stairs. The restaurant does not have upstairs seating so I knew the stairway didn't lead to just another dining room.

The moment I started up the stairs I knew I'd found what I was looking for. The creaking wooden stairway went straight up and was extremely narrow and dimly lit. With each upward step a heavier and heavier sense of dread weighed upon me. My worsening anxiety grew into a terror so intense that it almost forced me back down the stairs. But I continued to the top where I experienced a spell of relief. Momentarily.

Only a storage room and the restaurant owner's office were being used. Upon entering the storage room, I found it to be an ordinary, mostly empty area. Or, that is to say, empty in the physical sense, but not in the spiritual sense. Because something truly horrible filled that room—something of an unearthly nature. It was even worse than the feeling of the intense oppression on the stairs. The sensation was like being psychically choked. After only a few minutes I had to escape, so I fled back into the hallway, and thence to my dinner table.

Later I discovered that the Country House was formerly a roadhouse—a place in the country where people went to carouse, drink, and have illicit rendezvous. It wasn't the charming family restaurant with superlative food like it is today.

There are two stories related to the roadhouse era that might account for the current haunting. In 1958, a woman came into the roadhouse with a baby. She asked the bartender if she could leave her baby with him for a short time while she went off to take care of some business. On instructions from the owner, the bartender told the woman she couldn't leave the baby and she departed with her child. A short while later, the news came that the woman was killed in a car crash after leaving the roadhouse. She ran into a tree about a mile down the road.

Could it be this woman's presence which has left such an indelible mark of tragedy on the stairway and in the storage room? No one knows for sure, but a psychic reading has revealed that at one time in the past a woman had hanged herself on the upper floor and it is her spirit that has been occasionally seen at the window overlooking the parking lot.

Imagine the overpowering depression of a person about to hang herself, and how it would have dragged her down on her last trip up that long flight of stairs. Imagine the fearsome weight of guilt that would linger in the room where the suicide had been carried out. Such feelings could be so strong that they could be felt until this day—and maybe they are.

Red Lion Pub

Another place you are likely to find yourself dining with a ghost is the Red Lion Pub in Chicago. In fact, it's almost directly across from the Biograph Theatre where the ghost of James Lawrence (not John Dillinger) is seen in the alley. It had been a custom of mine to dine at the Red Lion even before I knew of its haunting and I'd actually experienced the ghost-noise without knowing what it was.

By an odd coincidence, I used to dine at the Red Lion on Sunday afternoons between three and four o'clock. One Sunday my usual dining was interrupted by a loud stomping sound overhead that crossed the ceiling the length of the pub. Thinking that it was only some unruly patron stumbling across the floor of the second floor bar, I simply went on with my meal. But it seemed very odd that I hadn't seen a single waitress or barmaid go up to or come down from the second floor. Nor had I heard the slightest noise from above—not a laugh, clink of glass, or anything else. Until now. So why, all of a sudden, were several of the restaurant staff rushing up to the second floor and returning with what seemed to be worried looks on their faces? Who had made the racket upstairs?

An odd circumstance; but I put it all aside as just one of those curiosities that never get answered. It wasn't until a number of years later that I learned what really had transpired that autumn Sunday afternoon in the Red Lion Pub.

I was watching a television special about ghosts when all of a sudden the Red Lion Pub was showcased. Sitting back in amazement, I listened as the owner of the pub explained how over the past several years they'd been plagued by this noisy ghost on the second floor. Time and again the sound of tramping footsteps were heard clumping overhead when no one was upstairs. Just to be sure, he and members of the staff always rushed to the second floor bar to make sure intruders hadn't broken in. Although they suspected they had a ghost upstairs, they didn't know whose it was or why it was there.

The irony is that this ghost is only heard on Sunday afternoons between the hours of three and four o'clock! So it turned out that the unusual series of events that I'd heard and observed on that afternoon so long ago did have a special meaning to it. I'm glad I finally was introduced to this ghost I might never have known.

But who is this ghost? There hasn't as yet been any explanation given as to its identity. Therefore, I'd like to offer a hypothesis. Taking into account that the Red Lion is almost directly across from the Biograph Theatre, might not the upper floor of the restaurant have been a perfect vantage point from which to observe the planned ambush of John Dillinger? Is it possible that someone who had witnessed the shooting had died suddenly and tragically? Maybe even a friend or loved one of James Lawrence, the man who had been killed in Dillinger's place? Just a hypothesis.

Castle Pub
The Ghost Who Drank Too Much

The Castle Pub is one of the few true Scottish pubs in the City of Chicago. Its walls are crammed with photographs of famous Scots from all areas of endeavour, ranging from soccer players to politicians. And since Scotland is where the best and purest Scotch comes from should it be any wonder that this pub has a ghost who still drinks the breath of the Auld Country?

Many years ago the pub was owned by a man named Frank Giff. Mr. Giff liked to imbibe a lot—morning, noon and night, as the saying goes. It would seem that a person with his taste for liquor had found heaven on earth by owning his own pub, having as vast a supply of alcohol as he could possibly want.

But as is so often the case—too much of a good thing can end up killing a person. Mr. Giff was found dead behind the bar one morning when his wife came down to open the pub. It was obvious that he'd drunk himself to death. Perhaps it was how he would have preferred to die. Although, it seems that even death hasn't killed his taste for the breath of the Auld Country and he may be one of the happiest ghosts on the other side—the other side of the bar.

Mr. Giff's wife eventually sold the pub. One of the first acts that the new owners undertook was a little face-lifting to the front of the building. They had workmen remove the plaque of an eagle which had been in storage out back and place it high over the entrance to the pub.

But when morning came it was found that the eagle had flown. Not far, just to the pavement below. The odd thing about it is that there wasn't any damage either to the front of the building or to the plaque itself—quite extraordinary when considering how far the drop was. Even if it had been done by someone playing a prank there still would have been some type of damage to the stucco in removing the plaque.

After a little investigation it was discovered that the plaque had been a favorite of Frank Giff's. But for some reason he didn't want it to ever be displayed on the outside of the building. And he still doesn't. Death hadn't changed his mind on the matter, at least that's what many believe.

A great many people also believe that Mr. Giff's belief in drinking hadn't changed either. The staff at the pub had seen the results of his continued nightly forays to the liquor cache which left a smaller supply of scotch than expected.

At first the new owner of the pub naturally thought that it was the help who had been sneaking snorts of scotch. But she never could find anyone copping a nip—anyone living that is. She'd never suspected that the culprit might be a ghost until one day a startling thing occurred before her eyes, the help's eyes, and in sight of several of the patrons. A shelf that held shot and wine glasses suddenly began to vibrate and a number of the glasses lifted up and flung themselves off the shelf and onto the floor.

Nothing like this had ever happened before. There hadn't been any large, rumbling truck or bus going by to cause the shelves to shake. There wasn't anyone outside working on the street with a jackhammer. There wasn't any construction going on anywhere nearby and there certainly hadn't been an earth tremor. Could it have been Frank Giff's ghost?

One way to find out would be to tape down some of the glasses on the suspect shelf in the event that the trembling recurred. That's what the owner did. The rattling of the shelf did happen again and a couple of the glasses did shake loose. This in itself was odd enough, but there was still the problem of the gradually depleting scotch from one of the bottles. Could this just be in the owner's imagination? After all, it's not easy to judge by sight how much liquor might have been removed from a bottle. What if a marking pen was used to measure the top level at which the scotch had been last left?

One of the bottles of Frank Giff's favorite scotch was duly marked and locked in a place accessible only to the ghost. In the morning when it came time to check the bottle it was found that a measurable portion of scotch had been removed. Frank up to his old tricks again?

Mr. Giff has other tricks he plays as well. In life, Mr. Giff was particularly partial to redheaded women. It appears that he still is. There is a special table in the pub where Frank used to sit after hours and apparently he still gravitates towards it whenever there's a good-looking redheaded woman there. Many women have reported a hand brushing their legs while seated at this table and having the sensation of a sudden chill. Frank sometimes "favors" blondes with a quick caress too, but never dark-haired women.

Frank Giff is a ghost who doesn't seem to know or care that he's dead, still carrying on as he did in life. When the new owners tried to put up the plaque of the eagle in the front of the building he didn't want done, he took it down. When Frank wants his usual night time shot of scotch he has it. When he sees an attractive redhead he lets her know he's around.

It seems that the Castle Pub would be the place to go for a little ghostly activity where more than one kind of spirit is served.

Strike!!

Bowling Ghosts

Bowling is one of the favorite pastimes for millions of Americans. Some of them enjoy the game so much that they even continue to play it long after they have died.

The location of this haunted site is in Brookfield, Illinois, which is just southwest of Chicgo. The site itself used to be the Sanctuary Restaurant but as of this writing is Alonzi's Villa. In the 1920s it was a bowling alley. And for some, it is still a bowling alley.

The wooden lanes that used to make up the bowling alleys are still in place but they are covered by the modern flooring. It was easier to simply lay another floor on top of the old lanes than to have them all torn out. Obviously, the former users of the lanes prefer it this way because some of them are still bowling here, much to the surprise of the diners at the present-day restaurant. It's somewhat unnerving to hear the sound of a bowling ball rolling beneath your table just as you're about to dip into your soup *de jour.*

There are other phenomena here as well. Disembodied voices have been heard by the owners and staff of the restaurant. But these aren't simply strange voices, they are voices of people who are known to the hearers; people who are not on the premises. Whoever this spirit is, it is of the mimicking variety, a very uncommon type of spirit. Not only does it mimic the voices of people known to the hearers it gets the hearers' attention by calling out his or her name. Imagine a ghostly voice calling your name, using the voice of a deceased loved one.

There hasn't been any explanation as to who this mimicking ghost is. Perhaps it belongs to a deceased performer who made his living doing impressions. As to who is making the racket on the bowling alleys: a ghost who still likes to bowl.

GHOSTLY GOINGS-ON IN CHICAGOLAND CEMETERIES

Resurrection Mary
Resurrection Cemetery

Chicagoland's most famous ghost is probably Resurrection Mary. She has even been featured on a national TV show about the paranormal.

No one knows for sure who Resurrection Mary is—or was. Since her ghost roams the southside of Chicago, which was a heavily Polish neighborhood, it is assumed that she was of Polish descent. Also being buried in Resurrection Cemetery is another good indication of Polish ancestry.

Resurrection Mary was allegedly struck by an automobile and killed one night while walking home from the Willowbrook Ballroom in suburban Justice, Illinois—ironically only a short distance from Resurrection Cemetery. As of this writing, the Willowbrook Ballroom is still operating, just as Mary is still attending her spectral dance and trying to hitch her way back home to Resurrection Cemetery.

Resurrection Cemetery is one of the largest cemeteries in the country, accommodating more than 130,000 grave sites. The grounds form a gigantic triangle bordered by Archer Avenue, Roberts Road, and 79th Street. It is most easily accessed from Interstate 55 by taking the First Avenue exit south to Archer Avenue. Follow Archer until you reach the cemetery.

The area around Resurrection Cemetery area is very dark and eerie. Even the street lights don't help and in some ways seems to add to the gloom. Knowledgeable drivers follow the route past the cemetery with eyes scanning the sidewalks in search of a blonde woman in a ball gown. Passersby were specially observant after a famous encounter in 1979.

A Chicago cab driver had just let off a fare in the suburb of Justice and was trying to get back on the highway. He was lost and looking for help. Spotting a young woman on the sidewalk ahead, he pulled over to ask directions. The woman said she'd help if she could get a free ride back to her home which was nearby.

The cab driver agreed and let the woman into the back seat. As they came up on Resurrection Cemetery, the woman called out to stop, this was where she was getting off. Turning to speak to the passenger, the cab driver found the back seat

The famous bars bent by Resurrection Mary. (Author's photo)

empty and no sign of the woman anywhere. He drove up and down the nearby streets in search of her but could not find the woman. Finally, the cab driver located a police officer and told his story, wondering if there had been any reports of a lost or missing woman roaming the area. There weren't any.

Since that night, there have been many sightings of this ghostly woman dressed in a white ball gown. Hoaxes are possible, of course, but some of the activity this spectral figure engages in is not possible for a human. She has been seen to pass through the bars of the cemetery fence, float above the ground, and disappear into thin air.

Mary's most amazing display involved leaving physical evidence. One night, a witness saw a woman in a white ball gown wandering aimlessly on the grounds of Resurrection Cemetery. The oddly-dressed woman stopped by the huge locked front gates and grabbed onto the bars as if attempting to get out. The witness called the police, thinking that someone had been locked in the cemetery and was trying to get out. When the police arrived they found no one in the cemetery and wrote the report off as a misidentification.

In the morning, however, when the gates to the cemetery were being opened, the impression of fingers were found seared into the metal bars where the ghost had grabbed them the night before. A hoax or fabrication was not possible because there was no way that the impression of fingers could be burned into metal showing the detail that these marks showed. I have seen pictures taken of these impressions and they are impressive.

Resurrection Cemetery is run by the Catholic Archdiocese of Chicago. When the ghostly finger impressions were found it was decided to remove them. The first attempt at removing the impressions and straightening the bars with a welder's torch was unsuccessful. It was determined that it would be best to simply remove the damaged area and replace that portion of the bars. Anyone can see this spot in the gate because it stands out from the rest of the unretouched bars. The official explanation for the damage to the bars is that a truck backed into the gate.

Sightings of Resurrection Mary continue and her fame grows. There has even been a song written about her by a local Chicago musician that can be played on the jukebox at a neighborhood bar which looks out at Resurrection Cemetery from across the street. The entire area is accessible to the public which may account for the numerous sightings of Chicagoland's most well-known ghost.

The Italian Bride
Mt. Carmel Cemetery

You might smell the scent of tea roses at this site. You may see a ghostly apparition or hear the whisper of saintly prayers. You will certainly be on hallowed ground.

The location is Mount Carmel Cemetery in Chicago and it is the grave site of Julia Buccola Petta who some have named the 'Italian Bride.' An impressive life-size statue stands above

her sarcophagus and on the side of her tomb is a picture of the deceased. In the picture, a young and saintly Julia is laid out in her coffin beautifully attired in her wedding gown.

Julia died as so many women unfortunately did in those days—in childbirth. In the early 1920s,

Statue of Julia Buccola Petta, the 'Italian Bride.' (Author's photo.)

giving birth was still a very risky undertaking and Julia was only twenty-nine years old when she died. But in Julia's case,

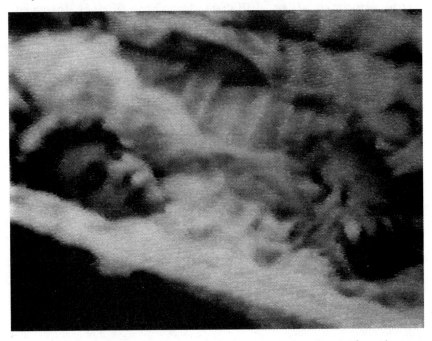

Picture of Julia Buccola Petta on her tomb. (Author's photo.)

the epitaph, "She died much too soon," might have had more truth than in most cases because it seemed that Nature agreed. Soon after Julia's death, her mother, Philomina Buccola, began experiencing distressing dreams about her deceased daughter. Night after night she'd have the same dream in which Julia would plead with her mother to have her grave opened and her body exhumed.

Finally, Philomina had to act. She sought permission from church and state authorities for an exhumation. Such permission is not easily gotten, despite what you see on television programs. Only under the gravest of circumstances are burial grounds allowed to be opened.

After six years of fighting to exhume the body, Mrs. Buccola was finally given permission to do so. In 1927, the grave site of Julia Buccola Petta was opened to the light and what was revealed was startling. After six years in the ground, not the slightest bit of decomposition had touched either the young bride's body or attire. Julia was the same perfect figure of a bride as the day she'd been laid to rest.

The question then becomes: what do we make of this? Was it indeed Julia's spirit calling out for this revelation to be uncovered to the world? If so, for what reason? Is it to imply her saintliness? Is it to announce that she had not truly been dead at the time of her burial but had fallen into a cataleptic state? Maybe it was so her child could have a chance to see what she'd looked like as a flesh and blood person rather than only in a mere photograph.

The mystery still remains. Julia was reinterred and the episode went down in local lore. There is a lingering physical reminder, however. At certain times, the strong fragrance of roses, Julia's favorite flower, can be detected near her grave site, even during the coldest of winter days when roses could not possibly be in bloom. Maybe Julia's message was simply one of warmth and good will.

Great Balls of Fire!
Bachelor Grove Cemetery

Bachelor Grove is a most extraordinary cemetery located directly south of Palos Heights, Illinois. It can be easily reached from Chicago by taking Highway 294 south, exiting at Harlem Avenue, and then heading east on 143rd Street until you reach the entrance to the cemetery.

Do not attempt to visit Bachelor Grove on Halloween! It will be strictly guarded by the police at every entrance. But you can visit here during the day any other time and if you are in search of Chicagoland ghosts this is a location you do not want to miss.

Bachelor Grove Cemetery was established in 1840 by German immigrants from the Bremen area of Germany. Little has changed in the surrounding environment since that time as Bachelor Grove is in the middle of a large forest preserve and the cemetery itself is located in a secluded area amidst deep woods.

From the minute you enter Bachelor Grove you know something is different. Even though the sun may be shining brightly there is an inescapable gloom that lingers over these woods. Any patch of brightness seems to be snuffed out by some overpowering force of dankness.

And the quiet here is piercing. There may be birds in the treetops and insects in the grass but you don't seem to be able to hear them. At night, the sense of foreboding is all the more extreme due to the lurking silence.

Many apparitions have been seen at Bachelor Grove Cemetery. The most famous is the disappearing house that has been witnessed by many people. The house is almost always described as an old-fashioned type of farmhouse, like those that existed at the end of the nineteenth century. This would be in keeping with the era in which the cemetery was in active use as such. But no one's been able to find records or evidence of a farmhouse existing here.

The house has been viewed in open daylight, as clear and as real as any other house you might see. But the next moment it's gone! And it's not easy to misplace a two-story farmhouse in the middle of a place where it would be quite conspicuous. Many people who have seen the house and then had it vanish on them did attempt to search for it; but no one has ever found it again.

Another startling apparition seen here is the phantom car. Most people describe it as a dark sedan of 1930s vintage. The sound of a loud engine and squealing tires is heard then a brief glimpse of a car is seen. Next there is silence again and empty air where the car had been.

The common belief is that this spectral vehicle belonged to Chicagoland gangsters who have driven here to dump off a victim or two into the murky lagoon that edges the cemetery grounds. For some reason they are reenacting the crime over and over again.

Not everyone sees the phantom sedan in the same place. Some people have spotted it on roads near the cemetery, making it seem that the car is blinking in and out of reality on its ghoulish cruise to Bachelor Grove.

Some people only hear the car while others—who were driving in their own automobile at the time—have had the sensation of being sideswiped by the phantom vehicle. They would pull over and stop only to find that they were alone on the roadway.

In connection with the spectral car have been spectral bodies. A number of witnesses have reported seeing bodies appearing on the ground near where one of these phantom autos have stopped. Moments later, the body would vanish, just like the car.

If you should dare to visit Bachelor Grove at night you may find yourself accosted by one or more of the famous ghost lights. Brilliant globes of blue spectral light have been seen bobbing and floating over the graveyard tombstones. In one case an individual was chased by one of the lights and was shoved over by another one.

Ghost lights are usually found associated with cemeteries and for some reason are usually blue in color. The scientific opinion is that the lights are explainable as the gaseous residue of decaying corpses escaping into the air. However, at Bachelor Grove, the corpses have all long since decayed. Another explanation for the Bachelor Grove ghost lights could be marsh gas coming from the nearby lagoon. But I have yet to see the glob of marsh gas that can chase or shove someone over.

There's even still more to witness in the way of the paranormal at Bachelor Grove. This is a relatively recent discovery, but it has been found that when you photograph the cemetery area you may develop a picture with more in it than you expected. Many photographs have come back with luminous hazy ectoplasm-like features in the background.

Some of these features appear to be in the shape of faces or have faces embedded in them. Also, if you photograph the tombstones themselves you may find these same features superimposed on them.

Why is Bachelor Grove such a haunted place? It is my belief that this spot was liberally used as a dumping ground for murder victims by the Chicago gangsters of the 1930s. The location is perfect for such grisly use: near enough to Chicago

Is this swirling mist at Bachelor Grove Cemetery a ghost?
(Author's photo.)

to be accessible, yet far enough away to be out of sight of all law enforcement authority. And when you take into account the secludedness of the area and the availability of a murky lagoon to toss victims in you have prime gangster burial ground real estate.

But this may be just one dimension to the Bachelor Grove phenomenon. How to account for the vanishing farmhouse? And what of all the ectoplasmic manifestations and the blue ghost lights? It seems that Bachelor Grove is much more than a gangster burial ground. This area may be some type of portal or gateway for spiritual beings, or maybe a holding place or prison for them. Whatever the answer, the variety and the intensity of paranormal activity taking place at this location mark it as one of the true hotspots of the supernatural.

Showman's Rest
Woodlawn Cemetery

The circus was coming to town! In 1918 this was a much greater, more stupendous event than in contemporary times even for big cities like Chicago which have so many other diversions to entertain people. Back in 1918, throngs of excited jubilant spectators would line the tracks to greet the arrival of the much anticipated circus train.

Chugging down the tracks from the east was the long, colorful train of the Hogenbeck Circus, carrying its menagerie of animals—some wild, some trained—and its assortment of performers. It would stop over for the night in Hammond, Indiana and then continue the trip into Chicago the next day to be met with an uproarious welcome.

The welcome never came. Tragedy did instead. While the train was laid over for the night on the side rails in Hammond so that everyone would be well rested for the big day on the morrow, another train came roaring down on it. It was a troop train which had somehow been switched onto the wrong tracks.

There was a thunderous crash. The ground shuddered as if a monstrous bomb had detonated. Tracks were torn up from their foundation and twisted into grotesque shapes. The sleeping cars of the circus train were crushed into one another—folded like an accordion—and the people inside were smashed lifeless or battered to death against the walls, floors, and ceilings. Some of the victims were hurled out of the windows by the force of the mighty collision.

Many of the animals were killed as well, helplessly trapped in their cages when the two trains crunched together.

For them, as well as for many of the humans aboard, there hadn't been any warning and death was instantaneous.

In all, fifty-six people were killed that night: high wire artists, strongmen, horse riders, acrobats and many more. Burial was made at Woodlawn Cemetery in Riverside, Illinois in a special section known as Showman's Rest. A troop of five stone elephants four feet high, mounted on separate stone pedestals, mark this area of the cemetery. Among the many new graves at Showman's Rest is that of circus fatman, Edward Kann, an individual who was so large that his burial took up two plots.

A troop of stone elephants stands guard at Showman's Rest where circus performers killed in a train wreck lie. (Author's photo.)

Are the performers who are buried at Showman's Rest truly at rest? Reports have come from many sources that tell of hearing the sounds of circus animals coming from the cemetery in the night. The great roars of lions, the trumpeting of elephants, and the whinnying of horses. But how could this be when there weren't any animals buried here?

The answer might lie several miles away in the nearby town of Brookfield, Illinois. This is where one of the largest zoos in the world is located—Brookfield Zoo. Could what seem to be the animal sounds associated with a circus be originating here? Are they transported upon the wind on favorable nights so that they seem to be arising from Showman's Rest?

The odds seem high that this is the case. It would seem to be a sensible conclusion. But sometimes when dealing with the paranormal we can't always go by common sense.

Statue of Death
Graceland Cemetery

A short distance to the north of Wrigley Field is Graceland Cemetery. Many famous Chicagoans are buried here: Marshall Field, Potter Palmer, Cyrus McCormick, Daniel Burnham (city planner), and William H. Hulbert, founder of baseball's National League. But it is the grave site of a relative unknown, Dexter Graves, which draws the most attention.

Situated near the entrance to the cemetery, the grave is vigilantly watched over by a frightening eight-foot-high bronze monument known as the Statue of Death. It was sculpted in 1909 by Lorado Taft and poses quite a fearsome sight. The ominous figure is completely draped in a flowing robe and only a portion of its grim face is visible in the folds of a deep cowl.

Popular belief is that this monument will not allow anyone to take a clear picture of it. You might want to take a close look at the picture of it in this chapter to determine if it's in focus or not. It seemed pretty clear to me.

Graceland Cemetery is also the site of the grave of young Inez Clarke, who on August 1, 1886, was struck and killed by a bolt of lightning. She was only nine-years-old at the time of her sudden death. Her grief-stricken family erected a marble statue to commemorate her life and placed it safely within a glass enclosure.

There have been many witnesses who can testify as to the paranormal events that seem to regularly occur at her grave on August 1, the anniversary of her death. They report seeing the glass enclosure above the girl's resting place fill up with an eerie white mist. Some people have seen the statue inside the enclosure cry while others claim to have witnessed it disappear.

Thus, if you happen to be in Chicago on August 1 you might want to visit

The 'Statue of Death,' marks the grave site of Dexter Graves. (Author's photo.)

Graceland Cemetery. It may be one of your best bets for sighting a ghost. And if it happens to be a Sunday, Graceland is only a short distance from the Red Lion Pub where their upstairs ghost walks on that day of the week between three and four in the afternoon. You can't ask for better punctuality from a pair of ghosts.

The 'Hungry Fence'
Mount Olivet Cemetery

Proceeding west from the John Hancock Building, you will find Mount Olivet Cemetery at 111th Street and Western Avenue. It's not the cemetery itself that is the center of strange activity but the fence that surrounds it. Over the years an extraordinary number of automobile accidents have occurred at one specific section of the fence, thereby winning for it the name of the 'Hungry Fence.'

While nothing of an occult nature has been unveiled to account for this odd phenomenon something of a visual peculiarity has. It has been suggested that the lengthy row of regularly-placed metal fence posts when continuously viewed from a passing vehicle can lead to a type of hypnosis causing susceptible drivers to lose control of their cars. Add to this the strobe-like effect of either a car's headlights or the rays from the sun flashing off the many shiny tombstones and you may begin to see how someone might be lured into a trance. Or then again, maybe the fence is imbued with some type of demonic force and seeks to attract victims to it.

A Shower of Roses
Holy Sepulchre Cemetery

Holy Sepulchre Cemetery is located on the extreme south side of Chicago, just south of Chicago Ridge. It is most easily accessed by following I-294 south, exiting north on Cicero Avenue and following 111th Street west. Holy Sepulchre is one of the largest cemeteries in Chicago and is not difficult to find.

Here is found the grave of Mary Alice Quinn. She was in most respects a saintly person. Unfortunately, she died at the tender age of fourteen and was prevented from performing all the many acts of charity and good will for which she wished she'd had time.

Mary Alice Quinn is not just another ghost story because since her death in 1935 many miraculous cures have been reported by people who have visited her grave site. People with all varieties of illnesses, ranging from the simplest complaints to life-threatening diseases, having claimed being healed due to the young ghost's intercession. Her reputation as a healer has grown to such an extent that visitors have taken to removing handfuls of soil from her grave as a sacred relic, causing the groundskeepers to constantly have to resod and repair the damage.

As she lay dying, Mary Quinn expressed her wish that she could alleviate the suffering in the world. She told her parents that after she died she would ". . . shower roses on the world." Many people believe that she does. Witnesses have reported smelling an overpowering fragrance of roses while at her grave site much like has been reported at the site of Julia Buccola Petta, the Italian Bride.

It seems that judging by the reports of miraculous cures and the scent of roses bestowed upon certain visitors to her grave site, Mary Quinn had fulfilled her desires in death which she was denied in life.

The Driverless Hearse
Resurrection Cemetery

You may have thought we left Resurrection Cemetery behind when we said good-bye and happy haunting to Resurrection Mary, but we're back again with a different apparition. Resurrection Mary has become such a well-known sighting now—even appearing on national television—that another ghostly phenomenon that occurs near her home cemetery is all but forgotten.

This apparition involves a driverless hearse—and old-time vintage horse-drawn hearse that is seen rushing out of the gates of Resurrection Cemetery and dashing wildly down Archer Avenue. Oddly enough, its destination is another cemetery: St. James of Sag Cemetery which was in use earlier in the 1900s.

Although it may seem odd for a hearse to rush from one cemetery to another—maybe he had taken a burial to the wrong graveyard—you also have to take into account that the vehicle is driverless. Maybe the ghost horse was simply following the route it knew best.

Many people have been startled by this odd sight as well as by peculiar occurrences at the huge mausoleum that stands on the grounds of Resurrection Cemetery. Frequently in the middle of the night organ playing has been heard and the lights in part of the building begin flickering wildly. When authorities are called to the scene there is never anyone there or any logical explanation such as faulty wiring or an electrical storm for the behavior of the lights.

But there's even more. Another manifestation is associated with this general area—the Sag Bridge ghost. It may even be the same driverless hearse that appears to bolt from Resurrection Cemetery and is merely being seen at another point on its journey crossing the Sag Bridge on Route 171.

At any rate, the vision was first seen by two visiting musicians from Chicago who were in Lemont, Illinois, to give a performance at the St. James of Sag parish church. The sound of hoofbeats awoke them in the middle of the night but when they went to the window to check on the noise they didn't see any horses. What they did see, however, was a black-haired woman dressed in white who was floating down the middle of the street. However, the horses that had been making the clatter then appeared, pulling a dark vehicle behind them. The shocked musicians watched in amazement as seconds later both the woman in white and the dark vehicle were swallowed into the road. No explanation has even been given as to who the white lady might have been or the reason for the appearance of the dark vehicle. The answers seem to have been swallowed into the ground with the apparitions.

Jewish Waldheim Cemetery

The Jewish Waldheim Cemetery is located at the intersection of Roosevelt Road and Harlem and just across the street from another Waldheim Cemetery. Jewish Waldheim has been reported to host a number of floating ghost lights and wailing noises in the night.

Robinson Indian Burial Ground

Another ethnic graveyard reputed to be haunted is the Robinson Indian Burial Ground which is located in a small but dense patch of woods on the outskirts of Chicago. It was a sacred spot to the Indians who had lived here before Chicago was built up and it still exists today although it is no longer used for burials. Witnesses have seen ghostly faces appearing in the dense underbrush which covers the burial plots and some people have seen faces materialize on the gray granite monument stone that was erected at the front of the burial ground to memorialize those who lie here. Witnesses have also reported seeing these faces show up on pictures that they've taken of the memorial stone.

HEAVENLY HAUNTS

The Spectral Monks of St. Ritas

November 2, 1960—All Souls Day. Halloween had just passed but it was still the season for hauntings. All Souls Day is the date in the Catholic calendar when the souls of the dead are remembered with special prayers.

This All Souls Day began like any other gloomy dark autumn day in Chicago. A number of parishioners were assembled in the pews of Saint Rita's Church at 63rd Street and Fairfield to remember and pray for those who had passed on. There weren't any official services taking place so the church was dimly lit and quiet. Whispered prayers and the snapping of lighted votive candles were the only sounds in the solemn setting.

The peace was soon to be shaken. The organ in the loft on the south side of the church began to wail, crying through the silence. Startled parishioners peered upward to see that the organ was playing on its own. No one was seated at the keys.

But the loft was not empty. Positioned on one side of the organ were three figures dressed in black monk's robes and on the other side three figures in white monk's robes.

Panicking, the parishioners leapt from their pews and raced to the side doors only to find that the doors would not open! Some force was holding them firmly closed.

Suddenly the six figures in monk's robes were down on the main floor, marching through the pews. The parishioners struggled even more frantically at the doors. Then a powerful cold wind swept through the church, and the doors blew open. At the same time, a ghostly voice whispered loud enough for all to hear, "Pray for me."

The parishioners piled out of the church. The monks had vanished. The church returned to normal. This was a one time occurrence of a supernatural event that was so awe-inspiring

and spiritually meaningful that its impression has lasted until this day. Who was the poor soul who had beseeched the prayers of the people in the church that day? Why has this apparition never appeared again?

Could it be that the troubled soul who had asked for prayers received them and was released from tribulation? Or had his or her plea come too late to be saved?

The Mysterious Nun

Because the site of the following account is a convent I have been asked not to give its name or a too precise description of its location. Privacy is highly regarded here and those in charge of the convent naturally have a very conservative outlook.

The general location is the extreme southwestern suburbs of Chicago. Nestled peacefully back far off one of the older less-used roads is a large long stone building. It is surrounded by vast lawns and is hidden behind many tall and leafy trees. You could drive past the convent without knowing it was there.

One driver, however, didn't drive past it. In fact, he was directed to the isolated location by his mysterious passenger in the back. The driver was a cabbie who had picked up his fare as she was hitchhiking along the road. It was indeed a very odd sight to see a nun in her full regalia thumbing a ride down a dark roadway.

A long winding driveway led up a moderately steep hill to the convent building. The nun told the cab driver that the turnoff to the driveway was just ahead and that this was her destination. The cab driver headed up the driveway but when he turned back to speak to his fare she was gone. Disappeared!

The cab driver was quite startled but continued the drive to the convent. When he reached the building he got out and knocked on the front door of the darkened cloister. The door was opened and he told his story to an incredulous housekeeper: how he'd picked up this hitchhiking nun, how she'd directed him here, and how she suddenly vanished.

One of the resident nuns overheard his story and as the cab driver described his phantom rider she recognized the person he was talking about. She invited the cab driver in and showed him a number of portraits of nuns who had previously lived at the convent.

Spotting a photograph of the nun he'd given a ride, the cab driver excitedly pointed her out. He was told that this woman had died many years ago and that he must have been mistaken. He knew he wasn't.

Of course, this is a familiar genre of ghost story. It usually involves a young man who picks up a young girl and takes her to her home. She vanishes when they reach their destination and the stunned driver goes up to the house in search of her. Her parents open the door, the young man describes the girl, and he is tearfully informed that the girl had been tragically killed years ago. He is also told that many young men have come to their door, having experienced the same phenomena as he had.

The difference between the hitchhiking nun story and the genre ghost story is that the story involving the convent actually occurred and there were three corroborating witnesses. Also, it wasn't a recurring event as in the fictitious stories. For some reason, the ghostly nun only needed the ride home that one night. Perhaps returning to the convent gave peace to her spirit.

The High-Spirited Priest

The following story originates from my home town, Joliet, Illinois. Catholic High School, overlooking the historic Des Plaines River, stands atop a bluff near the geographical center of the city. Known for its many state championships in high school football, Catholic High has also won a reputation for being haunted. Not only is the haunting well-documented with witnesses but the veracity of these witnesses is of the highest order—most of them being Catholic priests of the Carmelite Order.

The ghost himself is a priest—one Kellen Ryan. He entered seminary school in Ontario in 1953, went on to study history at St. Bonaventure, and was ordained a priest on May 27, 1965. He taught at Catholic High in Joliet from 1966 until his untimely death on March 6, 1972.

Kellen Ryan had a reputation at Catholic High as being a fun-loving type of person, even a prankster. He ran through the priory in the middle of the night, rousting his fellow clerics out of sleep with the cry that a priest had been beaten up in the rectory. When all the priests had been awakened and assembled in the rectory, Father Ryan turned on all the lights to reveal party decorations. It was his way of getting everyone to attend his surprise party.

Father Kellan Ryan

Father Ryan's parents lived nearby in Chicago—just a short ride to the northeast on Highway 55. On Saturday, March 5, 1972, he departed Catholic High to pay them a visit. En route back to the priory the next day, Kellen Ryan apparently fell asleep at the wheel of his car at about 4:10 a.m. and struck a utility pole. His vehicle burst into flames and the popular young priest of thirty-three died instantly.

Father Ryan did not waste any time in returning to the earth in ghostly form. On the evening of the day that Kellen Ryan died a fellow priest, Father John Koernschild, was drawn to the cafeteria by the blaring of the jukebox. Upon examining the jukebox, Father Koernschild found that there wasn't even a record on the turntable. Was this one of Father Ryan's old tricks? After all, when he was alive he used to like to play the jukebox when in the cafeteria. Seemingly, he still did even after death.

Father Ryan was replaced at Catholic High by Mike Nadeau. One month after Kellen Ryan's death Mike was suddenly awakened in the night by the ghost of the late priest who was sitting in a nearby rocking chair dressed in the garb of the Carmelite Order. Any thoughts that the vision might have just been a dream were dispelled the next morning when Mike found the March 7 printing of Father Ryan's obituary in the local paper lying on the floor. This in itself was extremely odd since Mike was in the habit of discarding newspapers that were over a week old and this one was a month old. But odder still was the fact that Mike's clock had stopped at 4:10 a.m. , the approximate time of Father Ryan's death.

Some months later the ghost appeared at the foot of the bed of Father Lucas Smith. Father Ryan was said to have assured him that he was happy where he was and that all was well. The ghost gave this same assurance to another one of the priests at Catholic High in the summer of 1977. Again positioned at the foot of the bed, Father Ryan issued his message of well-being to Father Bernhard Bauerle.

But Kellen Ryan wasn't finished with his visits. He made an especially noisy and memorable appearance on the tenth anniversary of his death. On March 6, 1982, an incessant knocking occurred on the back door of the priory followed by an urgent ringing of the doorbell. A priest hurried down to answer the door but found that no one was there. Of course, this could have been the work of a living prankster, but if the knocking and doorbell ringing had been done by a human why were there no footprints in the snow outside the priory door? Another significant point to note—the commotion at the door happened at about 4:10 a.m.

When he was an instructor at Catholic High, Kellen Ryan's classroom was Room 306. The lights to that room are frequently seen in the early morning hours when no one should be there. Many times priests have gone to Room 306 and turned the lights off only to see them turned on again only moments after they've left.

One of the janitors can attest to the presence of the late Father Ryan on the third floor. On one occasion a figure dressed in a Carmelite habit with the hood raised passed the janitor in the hall. When he didn't hear any footsteps and didn't get a clear response to his salutation, the janitor took a closer look under the hood but was startled to find that there was no face to be seen. Was it Kellen Ryan up to his usual pranks, using special effects that he couldn't have used in life?

Father Ryan's fame as a specter grew so large that students would gather in the high school on the anniversary of his death. On three straight occasions the burglar alarm went off on those nights in the office that used to belong to Father Ryan. An even more extraordinary occurrence in the ghostly exploits of Kellen Ryan is his appearance in Washington D.C. on the seventh anniversary of his death. He appeared at the organ of the Carmelite Hall and began playing shortly before the five a.m. service.

The ghost of Kellen Ryan is one of the most well-documented on record and perhaps one of the least publicized of all hauntings. Not only are the verifiable sightings of him numerous and the witnesses to his after-death pranks many but the manifestations are consistent, punctual, and seemingly purposeful.

Note the history of Father Ryan's appearances: the number that have occurred at 4:10 a.m. (the time of his death), the date when they take place (the anniversary of his death), and the prank-like nature of the manifestations which would be in keeping with his personality when alive. It would be extremely difficult to discount the fact of the late priest's returns especially when you take into consideration that most of his witnesses have been other priests, who as a group are usually of a conservative nature and not likely to fabricate wild stories.

It seems obvious that Kellen Ryan does not yet realize that he is dead. As you may recall, it is commonly believed among parapsychologists that one of the reasons ghosts remain on the earthly plane is that they aren't aware that they're dead. They realize that some change has occurred, but not precisely of what nature.

These earthbound spirits are almost always ones who have died tragically or suddenly. Kellen Ryan was driving from his parents' house back to Catholic High when he fell asleep at the wheel, crashed into a pole and was instantly killed. The last thing he would have remembered was driving in his car heading toward Catholic High. When his spirit was released from his body it mostly likely believed that the trip to Catholic High had been successfully completed and it attempted to go about life as normal, pulling the same old pranks, trying to reassure the other priests that all was okay. But it wasn't.

Until Father Ryan's spirit realizes and accepts its altered state the ghostly pranks will probably continue at Catholic High. At least he seems to still be having fun.

Roaming Monks and Maple Lake

These two haunted locations are situated very close together and may have more in common than their vicinity. Fairmount Cemetery and Maple Lake are both in what is known as the Palos Forest Preserve and are accessed off of Highway 171 just south of Willow Springs, Illinois. Several miles north of here is the famous Resurrection Cemetery.

Fairmount Cemetery is a most unusual burial ground because of its location and terrain. It is situated on a heavily-wooded uncommonly steep-sided hill for a graveyard, more suited for hiking paths and campsites rather than tombstones and mausoleums. Yet Fairmount Cemetery is a sizeable graveyard where burials are still made under the intense cover of foliage and in the always foreboding gloom. If you should visit this remote site you will most likely find the gates locked since sightseers are discouraged.

However, this will not necessarily prevent you from making a ghostly sighting. The manifestations that have been reported from Fairmount Cemetery are said to occur on the south side of the hill that makes up the graveyard. Thus, you would want to turn onto 95th Street on your driveby of this site. If you're very lucky you will get a glimpse of a group of brown-robed monks walking prayerfully down the slope amidst the tombstones. This is the only manifestation reported at this location and no explanation has been put forward as to who these monks are or why they're here. At any rate, this is a worthwhile site to visit for the atmosphere alone.

Also, almost directly across the street to the southwest is another haunted site, Maple Lake. Maple Lake is located amidst densely forested hills and is reached by a winding, treacherous hillside road. Exercise extreme caution when navigating 95th Street—especially in the dark. And this is a site you must visit in the dark. There is a convenient parking area that looks directly out on the lake but it is patrolled by the local police after dark and you may be asked to leave.

If you are allowed to stay, however, and keep your vision trained on the center of the small enclosed lake, you may be lucky enough to catch sight of the Maple Lake ghost light. It glows with a deep red radiance and hangs about fifty feet above the surface of the water. No explanation has been given as to why it appears.

Perhaps the ghost light marks the spot where someone had drowned in the lake either accidentally or otherwise. Perhaps it marks an ancient Native American burial ground. Perhaps the ghostly monks from the nearby cemetery are part of the mystery. Maybe they were martyred there at the hands of savages. We can only speculate at this time.

That the ghost light is real has been confirmed by numerous sightings. The obvious question as to the possibility of a hoax or misidentifcation then arises. To be a hoax, a person would have to somehow be able to make a brilliant red light appear over the center of the lake without revealing the source of that light.

Or could the light be some type of bizarre optical illusion cast upon the lake from the distance: a car's taillight or the glow from a radio tower? This seems unlikely because the lake is completely enclosed amongst forested hills. And even if the light could be caused by some distant reflection of a moving object like a car or train or airplane this couldn't explain how the red radiance could remain suspended in place for up to half an hour as it has been seen to do.

Somewhere there is an explanation for the Maple Lake ghost light—if not above the waters then perhaps below them.

GRAVEYARD BLUES
THE SINGING GHOST
OF JOLIET PRISON

In July 1932, the United States was in the midst of the Great Depression. On quiet summer evenings people would sit on their porches and listen to the crickets or just the wind sweeping through the elder and maple trees. Many didn't have jobs to get up early for in the morning so they'd often stay up late, dreaming under the night sky, hoping for the better days that they knew were just ahead.

People on Edgehill Street in Joliet, Illinois and in the surrounding neighborhoods were no different from the millions of other people who sat out on their porches at night. Maybe it was even a little more quiet here because there was woodlands and fields around them to hush the common city noises. Directly to the west of Edgehill Street was a vast field that belonged to the Illinois State Penitentiary at Joliet—the old Joliet Prison.

The old Joliet Prison—not to be confused with the modern day Stateville—is a mighty limestone structure with formidable walls and looming turrets. In design it is almost indistinguishable from a castle. Built in the mid 1800s, Joliet was one of the major maximum security prisons in the country and has housed some of the most notorious villains in history.

Joliet has also been home to a lot of nonentities, too: prisoners who had no family or friends and who died in prison with no one to claim their bodies. It is about one of these unknown prisoners that our story revolves, a person whose identity has never been uncovered for certain, although some claim to have solved the mystery of who this enigmatic singing ghost was.

My sources for this story are firsthand witnesses to the incredible events that transpired: my mother, father, and a number of neighborhood friends. The manifestation of the singing ghost literally occurred just outside my back yard where the penitentiary maintained a huge field for grazing cows to provide various dairy products for the prison's larder. Also on prison property was a deep limestone quarry which was equipped with high-powered sump pumps to keep it from filling with rainwater. Also on this land was the potters'

Thousands of people heard Joliet's singing ghost, including the two women pictured here telling their story to the sheriff.
(*Joliet Spectator* photo, 1932)

field cemetery where the unclaimed prisoners who died were buried. All of this was just beyond my back yard which ended at the barbed wire fence placed there by the prison!

I wasn't born until many years after the events in this story took place but besides the information I was given by my parents, I interviewed Elmer Ott, a newspaper reporter who covered the story for the *Joliet Spectator*. I also unearthed the continuing series of news reports on the event as they unfolded and were carried in the other local newspaper, *The Joliet Evening Herald*. The story also received national coverage for a time.

Like the singing ghost, this story flourished in July 1932 and then simply disappeared, finally to be resurrected again in these pages. I have done a great deal of follow-up research on this long-forgotten story and have come up with my own conclusion which differs from the one officially proclaimed in 1932.

When the full moon appeared in the sky on the sultry night of July 16 it was accompanied by the sound of singing. So say those who were first to hear the voice of the singing ghost. Others gave the exact time as 11:45 p.m.—just before the witching hour.

The mother of Stanley Dudek seems to have been the first to hear the singing since the cemetery was almost directly outside her back yard (my family's house was a little farther down the street). It was 11:30 p.m. when Mrs. Dudek first heard the beautiful baritone voice singing what sounded like Latin hymns from the Catholic Mass. She and her daughter Genevieve ventured out into their back yard to investigate. Taking a flashlight, they shined it on the exact spot from which the singing was coming, but saw nothing.

The next night Stanley Dudek and his father George, who had been away the night before, also heard the singing and thoroughly searched the cemetery out back but didn't find anything either. News of the singing ghost quickly spread and those in the neighborhood who had also heard it now realized that it wasn't just someone's loud radio they had been hearing. There was a ghost in the penitentiary's potters' field!

One night at the beginning of the ghostly episode a local fisherman was taking a short cut from his day's angling and chanced to cross the potters' field. This was before news of the ghost had become widely known. As the fisherman headed through the graveyard, a voice asked him, "Any luck today?"

Turning to answer, the fisherman found that he was completely alone . . . in the middle of a prison cemetery at night! Terrified, he fled as fast as he could, flying across the open field, finally catching his foot in a cow's hoofprint and falling. He said that his momentum had been so great that he rolled the rest of the short distance to the road bordering the field.

News of the specter in the prison field graveyard spread even farther and soon people from all over town were driving to the area in hopes of hearing the Latin hymns of the singing ghost. Lines of cars filed up Woodruff Road and turned into the prison field where industrious youth of the area directed them to parking places. The procession started early in the evening and usually stopped at around 11:00 p.m. because the ghost traditionally began singing around midnight. In fact, people in the crowd would count down the time until the performance would begin.

"Twenty minutes to twelve . . ."

"Seven more minutes to go . . ."

"Almost time."

"Midnight!"

After ten days, the singing ghost had become well-known throughout Chicagoland, bringing in thrill seekers from Chicago, Indiana, and the nearby communities of Plainfield, Lockport, Aurora, and Rockdale. People even made the trek from as far away as Missouri to hear the ghost's singing. According to Joshua Jones of Sickle Center, Missouri, "Folks in my town read of this singing specter in the newspapers but they won't believe it until they hear from me." He was sent to report on the reality of the singing ghost.

At first the visitors to the ghostly scene numbered in the hundreds, now they were coming in the thousands. A site where you can hear a singing specter perform nightly almost without fail is rare; and a genuine ghost whose existence cannot be denied is unique. From the beginning searchers attempted to uncover either the whereabouts of the ghost or someone pretending to be the ghost. And from the outset all such attempts were utterly futile. People began accepting the genuineness of the ghost only once all attempts to prove it a hoax had been made and had failed.

Whenever the singing would begin a deputation would be sent out to track down the source. The searchers were always left standing in the middle of an empty field, frustrated. People looked behind bushes, in trees, even below ground for

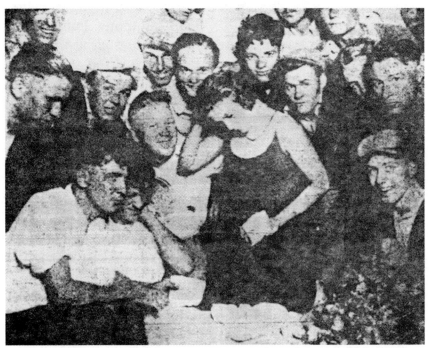

Witnesses went directly to the grave site to hear the singing ghost as shown in this photo. (*Joliet Spectator* photo, 1932)

hidden caverns. Nothing! They looked for wires and loud speakers and microphones and still found nothing. Yet the singing persisted night after night. A low, mournful chanting of Latin hymns. What else could it be but a genuine ghost?

Each night now thousands of people drove to the field and climbed the hill to the once lonely burial ground. People sat on the flat grave markers, spread blankets in the grass, and brought thermoses of coffee. All across the dark field ghost stories were told and retold as the expectant ghost hunters awaited the rising of the spectral voice. Young and old came to the site, believers and skeptics. It was splendid entertainment and a true-to-life ghost story in which everyone was participating.

On one occasion, a Catholic priest was ushered to the graveyard in full vestments, carrying a copy of the *Rituale Romanum,* to perform an exorcism over the troubled grounds. The exorcism is a little known fact and something that I believe has great bearing on this manifestation. Imagine the spookiness of the setting. As votive candles glow amidst the grave markers and holy incense wafts on the still air, the commanding voice of a Catholic priest calls out in ancient Latin for the troubled spirits to leave this place and never return again!

Eventually, the singing ghost began to miss his nightly performance. And when he did sing it was much later in the night, as late as four a.m., long after the thrill seekers had given up and gone home. But the faithful would stay, huddled in blankets and drowsing in the chill predawn air, to be rewarded by the much-delayed singing. According to them, the ghost was affronted by the purely thrill seekers and disturbed by all the commotion. He preferred quiet attentive listeners as he sang his prayerful hymns and did not like noisy hooligans.

Officials of Joliet Prison had another explanation for the ghost's sudden loss of voice. They had solved the month-long mystery of the singing ghost, declaring that the Latin hymns sung in the night had come from the throat of a very-much-alive convict. The lead story in the *Joliet Evening Herald* for July 29, 1932 began:"The Singing Spectre of Potter's field on 'Monkey Hill' is only an Irish-German prison trusty singing in jubilation as he awaits a parole scheduled to come within two weeks."

The trusty's name was William Lalon Chrysler who had been sent to Joliet Prison after being convicted of larceny in nearby Cook County. He had served four years of a one to ten year term. According to warden Frank C. Whipp, the thirty-three-year-old Mr. Chrysler had been put in charge of late night inspection of the sump pumps in the quarry about three weeks before. Mr. Chrysler was a happy type of person, noted for his fine singing voice.

According to the 'ghost,' in his confession, he sang Lithuanian folk songs in English to relieve his monotony down in the depths of the quarry and also because he was scared of being there alone. He also said that he didn't know any hymns in Latin but, after being told by one of the guards about the commotion his singing was raising, tried to mimic church music to please the crowds. Chrysler also affirmed that when people came out looking for him in search of the ghost he would simply evade them by hiding in a bush.

Prison officials stated that the bare stone walls of the quarry in which Chrysler was stationed were perfect sounding boards for enhancing and throwing his baritone voice up to the hilltop more than a quarter of a mile distant. They added that if there was a northerly wind his voice would be carried directly to the potters' field cemetery where the people gathered to hear it. On nights when the wind wasn't favorable Chrysler's singing wouldn't carry to the cemetery. Thus they closed the case of the singing ghost of potters' field.

That is the official story. And as we all know the official story is not always or even usually the true story. But in this case the official explanation was so convincing that it was accepted by most people. It seemed that the singing ghost had been put to rest for all time.

That was in July 1932. On looking back however we find that there are a number of questions that still aren't answered. But more than that some of the answers that were supplied back in 1932 and almost universally accepted are not backed up by facts. I believe that the authorities were involved in a cover-up.

The obvious question must be dealt with first. Why would prison officials and others in powerful positions want to perpetrate a cover-up? What was their motive? One answer is that it was an attempt to reestablish authority on the part of prison officials and law enforcement authorities. For an entire month prison officials had had to deal with thousands of people encroaching on prison property. The barbed wire fence that surrounded the prison field was breached and broken and what had been a pasture for cows had been turned into a vast parking lot. This couldn't be allowed to continue.

Not only was both the prison's authority being impugned but so was that of the local police and the sheriff's department. At the outset there hadn't been any lawbreaking, with the exception of trespassing, associated with this ghostly affair. But as the story became more widely known and the numbers of visitors to the site grew into the thousands, it attracted a rowdy element that was disrespectful of neighborhood property and far more interested in causing trouble than witnessing a ghostly manifestation.

During the final days of this event, some of the less upstanding members of the neighborhood youth began a car parking racket. They started extorting parking fees from ghost hunters by threatening the motorists with broken windshields if they didn't pay up. Clearly, the situation had deteriorated from the first days when neighborhood kids were helping direct traffic.

Since the prison officials couldn't stop the ghost from singing they did the next best thing and discredited it. William Lalon Chrysler would provide the perfect solution. They named him as the unsuspecting ghost and disbanded the throngs from their fields forevermore. William Chrysler certainly wasn't about to dispute prison officials; he was due for parole in a couple of weeks.

Where does the official story fall short of the facts? According to the official story, Mr. Chrysler was at the bottom of a quarry singing his tunes which were transported to a nearby hilltop about a quarter mile away. He must have had a light with him which would have been seen by someone in the pitch black night. Remember, people were actively searching the entire area for the source of the ghostly singing!

Another inconsistency is William Chrysler's own testimony. He stated that when people came looking for him he'd simply hide behind a bush. In an actively worked quarry? A quarry is nothing but pure rock! And even if a bush should somehow sprout in the midst of a quarry it surely wouldn't provide an adequate hiding place for anyone.

Another problem with the official story is how Chrysler's voice could have been transported over such a distance. The 'quarry-as-a-sounding-board' theory does not make sense. According to magicians and ventriloquists who were interviewed at the time, they agreed that the art of ventriloquism—which Chrysler did not possess—would have been necessary to project a voice over such a distance. They added that even if Chrysler was a master ventriloquist he still couldn't have performed such a feat at night over that great of a span of land.

And finally: Why did no one ever hear the sump pumps? According to the official story, manning the sump pumps was why Mr. Chrysler was in that quarry. How is it that his singing could be heard but the loud noises made by sump pumps couldn't?

But there remains one fact that must be accounted for: the singing ghost was not heard again after William Chrysler's "confession." But also, neither was it heard again after the exorcism performed in the potters' field graveyard by the Catholic priest. Could it be that the exorcism was successful and that the ghost of the troubled convict was released from his prison on the earthly plane?

Whatever the reason, the singing ghost is no longer heard in the old prison graveyard. Is it because William Chrysler was indeed the ghost? Is it because the exorcism by the Catholic priest had been successful? Or could it simply be that the voice of the singing ghost is no longer heard because people stopped listening for it?

A PHANTASMIC TOUR OF CHICAGOLAND

Rosemary's Baby and Hull House

Goodwill was certainly much in abundance in the soul of Jane Addams. Jane Addams was the illustrious social worker in the late nineteenth and early twentieth centuries who was responsible for many of the child labor laws that had been enacted during that period. She did a great deal to change and better many people's lives.

In 1889, Jane Addams and a fellow social worker, Ellen Starr, rented a house at 800 South Halsted Street in Chicago. The house had been built in 1856 by noted architect Charles G. Hull and has since become known as Hull House. Ms. Addams used this house as a haven for young girls and little by little rented and renovated other buildings in the surrounding area. Eventually, she developed an entire complex consisting of schools, day care facilities, and even a gymnasium. Her many achievements can be read about in her two books detailing her work at Hull House.

But there's an odd legend also associated with Hull House. Near the Hull House neighborhood there was a dance and music hall frequented by many of the local people. One night in 1913, a suave mesmerizing stranger attended the festivities and astounded the patrons with his amazing dancing ability. He also charmed the ladies with his hypnotic personality. It is said that he charmed one of the young ladies off the dance floor and into bed in a nearby hotel. By the time she discovered she was pregnant the mesmerizing dancer had disappeared from the face of the earth.

Some of the people who had attended the dance hall that fateful night believed that the stranger may literally have been the Devil. Rumors spread that while engaging in one of his more gymnastic dancing feats, the dark stranger had momentarily bounded out of one of his shoes, revealing a cloven hoof! This, of course, was never officially verified.

At any rate, the unfortunate woman had her baby and was allowed to care for it within the privacy of the Hull House walls. More rumors claimed that the baby had many of the features one would associate with a father such as his: horns, a tail, and cloven feet. None of this is substantiated, but it makes an interesting story.

Jane Addams

Hollywood thought it was more than just an interesting story because it is believed that the 1960s horror classic, *Rosemary's Baby*, was based on this legend. Adding to the likelihood of this is the number of Chicagoland natives who were associated with the making of the film.

Regardless of the veracity of this legend of the Devil's dance hall visit, the main mansion of Hull House—which is all that exists today—has been the site of a ghostly apparition. Lights have been seen to go on and off by themselves inside the gloomy old building, which now houses a museum, and a strange figure has been observed looking out of one of the upper-story windows long after the building had been locked. No one knows whose ghost this is, nor even if it belongs to "Rosemary's baby."

There have been many witnesses at this location because, even though the house itself is steeped in gloaming, it edges the University of Illinois-Chicago campus. In the mid 1960s, the sprawling Hull House complex was levelled for the building of the campus. Students often walk to and from classes or the library in the vicinity of Hull House and are one factor in the frequency of ghostly sightings.

The Hull House mansion and museum can be visited during the day and you may see more than expected.

In the story about Hull House and its ghost we touched upon ghostly lore—stories that are more fiction than fact. It is more likely to be fiction than fact that the Devil visited a dance hall and impregnated one of the women. In this section we are going on a whirlwind tour of Chicago and the entire Chicagoland area, sweeping up ghostly stories and legends as we fly. Sightings have been made at each of these locations but in some cases on a very irregular basis. If you are travelling to these sites in search of a ghostly apparition your chances for a sighting will be very hit-and-miss.

DOWNTOWN CHICAGO

An Antique Shop Where You May Get More Than You Bargained For

Chicago is noted for its mixture of storefronts and residential areas. It's not unusual to pass rows of towering brownstone apartments and then come upon a convenience store. Often the owner of the commercial property will live upstairs over the store, in a back room, or in an apartment just down the block.

Belmont Avenue is typical of this mixture of commercial and residential buildings. One of the stores started out as a place of residence but soon after construction the woman who owned it was murdered. The house was sold and the new owner turned the downstairs into a store. The location, however, seems to be a tragic one because yet another catastrophe befell the new occupants when a fire in the attic killed four people.

The storefront at 806 West Belmont Avenue became Victorian House Antiques. The antique shop today is cluttered with furniture and bric-a-brac from dusty days gone by. Romantically speaking, it would be hard to envision a better location for a haunting than an antique shop.

The tiny store is haunted by the spirits of those whose lives were so abruptly ended here. Visitors to the store have seen fleeting apparitions passing amongst the closely crammed together furniture. Faces appear behind the dull glow of mirrors and creaking sounds are heard coming from various nooks. Then there are the sounds from the attic—cracking floorboards accompanied by groaning noises. But it's far too late now to do anything for the four who had died there, forever trapped with no way of escape.

A person has to wonder how many ghosts actually haunt this site. Have outside ghosts been imported to this antique shop? It is commonly accepted among parapsychologists that furniture can be haunted and that the spirit who has attached itself to it will travel with that piece of furniture to wherever it may be transported. This is similar to the poltergeist phenomenon in which the violent activities travel to different locations with the human victims when they try to flee.

It's always wise to attempt to find out some of the history of a piece of pre-owned furniture before you buy it. You might want to know if someone had died in that chair you're about to buy. Numerous ghosts have been seen still rocking in their favorite rocking chair. Would you want to take one of these home with you? You may get more than you paid for.

The Hand Print in the Firehouse Window

It is April 18, 1924, in one of the city's old-fashioned neighborhood firehouses—Good Friday. The crew at the firehouse at 13th and Oakley is busy cleaning up the station: washing down the trucks, mopping the floors, and cleaning the windows. Suddenly, the alarm goes off and all work is dropped as everyone races to the fire trucks and his appointed place on the vehicle. The crew from the fire station arrive on the scene of a very severe blaze. They are soon joined by others from nearby stations. It takes hours to finally bring the fire under control and eight firefighters lose their lives, including one from the station at 13th and Oakley—Frank Leavy.

Exhausted and in deep despair after the loss of one of its members, the crew returned to the fire station. Mops were still lying on the floor where they'd been hastily dropped when the alarm had sounded. Buckets of once soapy water that had long ago lost their suds stood beneath partially cleaned windows. Then a most startling discovery was made. What looked like a hand print had been left in one of the windows by the man who had been cleaning it—a hand print that was now indelibly pressed into the glass!

Everyone in the firehouse gathered around the miraculous window. It was the window that Frank Leavy, the man who had been killed in the fire, had been cleaning before the alarm went off. Experts from the Pittsburg Glass Company were called in to determine if the print was actually just a flaw in the glass. When they couldn't give a definite answer, Fire Department officials decided to attempt to remove the hand print with special cleaners. This didn't work.

The print remained in the glass for exactly twenty years. On the twentieth anniversary of Frank Leavy's death a paperboy tossed a newspaper through the famous window, shattering it and destroying the evidence. This much is true—an odd coincidence to say the least.

Field Museum

Still in the City of Chicago, we now visit the Field Museum. You will recall that on the bridge near the lagoon in the back of the Museum of Science and Industry is where the ghost of Clarence Darrow has been seen. But there's also a mystery inside the nearby Field Museum.

On display on a lower level is an ancient Egyptian exhibit. Included in the exhibit are mummies thousands of years old. It appears that one of these mummies—named Hawrar —still has some life in him and can get around.

According to security officers, on more than one occasion Hawrar's sarcophagus has been found off its platform and lying several feet away. No longer in an upright position, it would be flat on its back. On nights when this occurred a noise like a loud shout is said to be heard coming from the subterranean exhibit.

As bizarre as this story might seem, the Field Museum has acknowledged its accuracy and had at one time even made note of the happening in its ancient Egyptian exhibit brochures.

Urban Totem Pole

A similar type of attraction can be experienced a few miles north of the museum on Lake Shore Drive. Finding the appropriate exit to locate this site will require something like ESP but if you keep your eyes toward the lake and go slowly enough you will spot the Belmont Harbor Drive turn off. Take this to the east and you will soon find yourself facing a most unusual sight for a metropolitan area—a totem pole. Some people think that it's a most unusual totem pole.

Local lore states that the totem pole moves; one day it is facing in one direction, another day it is turned at a slightly different angle. The top character is supposed to be imbued with a powerful Indian spirit force that keeps it ever vigilant. So, if you're ever in this area, keep your eyes on this totem pole —it may be watching you!

The Phantom Lighthouse of Lake Michigan

Since you're standing along the edge of Lake Michigan at this site, it might be worth your while to gaze out into the night time waters. There are a number of lighthouses placed out on the jetties, but one that is no longer there but can sometimes still be seen anyway. There have been reports of people having seen the illumination from a phantom lighthouse which is no longer operational. Apparently it is still being tended by a spectral keeper. You might want to keep on the lookout for it.

The John Hancock Building

Travelling a short distance south of the Belmont Harbor Drive location, you will find the famous John Hancock Building in the heart of Chicago. Most people are unaware that this building sits on cursed land.

Back in the very early days of Chicago, an eccentric named Cap Streater decided to build his own settlement on the edge of town. He chose a location on the shore of Lake Michigan and solicited everyone to dump any and all garbage on this spot. Naturally there was a lot of people willing to dump a lot of garbage for free and in a short time Cap Streater found himself sitting upon a great peninsula of garbage that extended into the Lake.

The garbage pioneer laid claim to this mass of refuse and named himself Mayor of Streaterville. City officials of Chicago finally took note of what was happening offshore and decided that this huge garbage heap could become valuable if properly filled in and landscaped. So they evicted the Mayor of Streaterville from his domain and annexed the garbage dump to the City of Chicago. Cap Streater's only recourse was to pronounce a curse upon his lost land.

Over the years, a few odd deaths have occurred here. A young woman plunged over a hundred floors from the John Hancock Building to her death on the sidewalk below. She was totally naked at the time and no explanation was ever found as to the cause of her leap.

There was also a strange birth—Anton Lavey, former circus entertainer and founder of the Church of Satan.

Water Tower

Practically everyone knows about the Great Chicago Fire of 1871. Between October 10 and 12, 1871 four square miles of the heart of downtown Chicago was destroyed by a fire that couldn't be stopped. Driven relentlessly from the southwest toward the northeast, the inferno killed at least two hundred fifty people and came to an end only when it reached the shores of Lake Michigan and could travel no further.

Only a single structure was left standing in the very center of downtown—the Water Tower. Massively constructed of yellow limestone, the Water Tower is shaped much like a lighthouse and stands about the same height. It is an elegant, graceful structure, a symbol of the past.

The Great Fire of 1871 fed voraciously on the thousands of wood structures which made up most of the city at that time. The Water Tower was the only building made of stone which was why it survived the fiery holocaust. It isn't difficult to imagine terrified people seeking refuge in the only building that would repel the mighty flames overwhelming the city. Unfortunately, the billowing clouds of smoke couldn't be kept out of the structure. While there are no records to document if people died seeking refuge in the Water Tower there are apparently ghostly figures with tales to tell.

Strange figures have been seen in the narrow windows far above the ground in the Water Tower. A couple of the specters seem to be hanging by their necks from ropes. Could these be the spirits of people who had chosen to meet death by killing themselves rather than being suffocated by the inpouring of clouds of smoke from the monstrous fire all about them? No one knows who the ghostly figures are or why they are there.

Is it also an odd coincidence that the Water Tower resembles the Tower of Destruction card in a tarot deck including the hanging figures?

A Night On the Town

Returning to the heart of Chicago, there are rumors about the Chicago Theatre being haunted. In the manner of many old-time theatres there is an underground pond beneath the floor which once was used to operate the hydraulic system for the stage. There are many gloomy places down here that a ghost might prowl. It is said, however, that this male ghost does most of his wandering in the balcony.

Divine Intervention or Ghostly Grace?

Since we're once again back in the center of Chicago there's another site we do not want to bypass. It is the Holy Family Church and, like the Water Tower, it survived the Great Fire of 1871. It was quite miraculous that Holy Family Church survived because it wasn't built to be impervious to fire as had the Water Tower. The fire simply went around the church and left it standing. It too is reputed to be haunted.

THE OUTSKIRTS OF CHICAGO

Field of Horror

O'Hare International Airport, constructed on land formerly called Orchard Park—ORD in airport terminology—is acclaimed one of the busiest airports in the world. Most major airlines fly from here and there are hundreds of arrivals and departures each day, weather permitting. On one particular day it would have been better if there had been one less departure.

It was May 25, 1979. The day was bright and warm with only fair weather clouds in the sky. There wasn't any hint of a problem on the American Airlines DC-10 jet that was roaring down the runway that late afternoon. It was only seconds later, however, that something terrible went wrong. While the jet was still climbing it suddenly banked sharply to the left, assuming a vertical position to the ground. It then nose-dived the remainder of the way downward into a thunderous crash. In what was then the worst crash in U.S. aviation history, 273 people died instantly in a hellish fireball.

The cause of the crash was quickly determined. One of the DC-10's engines had dislodged shortly after takeoff and was found on the runway onto which it had plummeted.

The jet crashed in a field just beyond the runway and exploded into thousands of pieces, spewing fiery debris over acres of ground. No one survived. The task of retrieving the dead from the smoldering—in some areas still burning—wreckage was gruesome. Tiny pennants were stuck into the ground across the littered field to mark the locations of dead bodies, punctuating a tragedy of horrific proportions.

Soon after the remains of the dead and the debris had been cleaned away, the field where the crash occurred was plowed over and sown with new grass. It was to be a memorial site to those who had died there. But it is believed by many that the spirits of the victims of the airline crash that fateful day still linger in that cursed field, memorializing it in their own way. The sounds of moans and screams have been heard rising from here. So too has the noise of a crashing jet. Death had come so suddenly to the unfortunate passengers of the doomed flight that many of them may not be aware that they have died, as is the case with many ghosts.

While eerie sounds have been heard coming from the crash site, an odd apparition has been reported from inside the gate of the terminal from which the ill-omened flight originated. Witnesses claim to have seen a ghostly figure at one of the pay telephones near the lounge. He would be seen finishing a conversation on the phone and turning to depart. But after his first couple of steps he vanishes. Could this be the ghost of a man who had just completed a last telephone call to his loved ones? If only he'd stayed behind and had missed that flight!

Argonne National Laboratory

Between the cities of Lemont and Darien, Illinois, is the location of Argonne National Laboratory where the brightest minds in the world work on the most complex scientific experiments of the day. It is a virtual city hidden away in the depths of the dense forest. Visiting this site is like entering another world where even the people seem different, probably due to their outrageously elevated IQs. You cannot visit here without a special security pass so if you're in the area don't expect to drop in.

However, the area that interests us is the forested region that surrounds the laboratory. Cass Avenue, a secluded public road winds through it, can be accessed directly off of Highway 55, going south. When driving this road in the darkest part of the night you can see glowing eyes staring at you from the underbrush. If you stop and look closely you may spot one, two, or even a herd of the famous ghost deer that freely roam the area.

These deer are there, they do exist, and they do appear to be ghosts with glowing eyes. They are not ghosts, however. The legend is that these glowing deer are the results of experiments conducted at the nearby Argonne National Laboratory. The official story is that they are simply a herd of white deer that long ago were imported into the area. In any event, they make quite a spooky sight along the dark and secluded roadway in the deep of the night.

A Night At The Opera

Follow Highway 14 toward the northwest from Chicago for several miles and you will come to the small town of Woodstock, Illinois. In the nineteenth century, Woodstock was a rural town set in the midst of vast acres of lush Midwestern farmland. Its nearest neighbor was Harvard, Illinois, about twenty miles to the north and Crystal Lake about twenty miles to the south. The drive to Woodstock through the sprawling farmland was particularly spooky in the autumn when the sullen air was hazy with smoke and the harvested fields were dressed with haystacks.

Woodstock was something of a cultural center for the rural area and boasted an often-used opera house which was built at the end of the nineteenth century. Patrons would journey from as far away as Milwaukee to attend a show, but most of the audience came from the surrounding farming communities. Occasionally among the audience is one particularly noteworthy guest—Elvira.

Elvira is the female ghost who haunts the Woodstock Opera House and has been doing so for at least ninety years. She was a performer at the opera house in its early days, shortly after the theatre had been constructed. No one knows for certain why, but in 1903 Elvira hung herself, tragically ending her earthly life and abruptly beginning her existence as a ghost.

Elvira still attends the opera at the Woodstock Opera House not as a performer but as a patron—and critic. When she views a performance she does not like, the lights will flicker and go out and eerie noises will echo throughout the building. Her apparition has been frequently seen at the theatre and has become such a faithful patron that the management has reserved a seat especially for her: DD 113.

The Woodstock Opera House is highly recommended as a site for ghost-seeing. Of course it is also an excellent place at which to take in a good opera. While enjoying the music, however, be sure to take frequent glances at seat DD 113. If you see a well-dressed lady there in nineteenth-century attire, you should hope that she has a pleased expression on her face and is enjoying the show.

THERE'S NO PLACE LIKE HOME ... EVEN IF YOU'RE DEAD

Pullman Mansion

George Mortimer Pullman was an engineer who invented the Pullman sleeping car in 1863. It was a revolutionary accomplishment which forever changed the way that people travelled by train and made George Pullman an extremely wealthy man.

A factory city called Pullman, Illinois, was founded on the southside of Chicago in 1880 and is located directly off Highway 94 at 111th Street. The crowning edifice of this town was the glorious Pullman mansion. Informal tours of the mansion used to be given, but one location that the tour did not visit was the cellar. Legend has it that the body of George Pullman, who died in 1897, has been kept perfectly preserved in the cellar, floating in a vat of formaldehyde. Unfortunately, I have not met anyone who has seen this amazing sight.

A Castle in Beverly

Beverly, Illinois is a suburb south of Chicago. Coming south from Chicago, the best way to reach Beverly is by way of I-90/94, exiting west on Mannheim Road. It is a very small community of quiet old-fashioned neighborhoods but in the middle of this staid little village is an impressive Irish castle constructed of mighty limestone blocks.

The castle was built in 1886 by architect Robert Gibbons as a present for his wife. She was to come over from Europe to live in it and he hoped it would make her feel more at home. Reports are that his wife didn't like the castle so it was sold.

In 1890, the castle was made into a girls' school, and it may be from this period that our first ghost originates. On more than one occasion a little blonde girl dressed in 1890s attire has been seen in the castle.

In one report from 1960, a night watchman while on his rounds came upon a little girl in old-fashioned clothes and he pursued her through the house. When the girl reached the front door she passed through it without opening it. The watchman was close behind her and when he rushed outside he found that the girl had vanished. What made this particularly mystifying was that there was a blanket of newly-fallen snow on the ground and there were no footprints to be seen anywhere.

On another occasion there was a gathering being held in the building and the little girl in the old-fashioned attire was spotted by several of the people in attendance. When the girl was confronted by one of them, she remarked that all that she wanted was to get back home. Then she vanished.

The girl's identity has never been established and there is no evidence of foul deeds having been perpetrated at this location. Perhaps the girl was just homesick and wanted so desperately to be back with her family that these longings have remained in the atmosphere over the decades.

Since 1947, the castle in Beverly has been the site of a Universalist Unitarian Church. One of the recent pastors of the church relates some odd experiences he's had in the old, cavernous building in the quiet hours. From time to time, he's heard the sound of a party going on in one of the downstairs meeting rooms. When he goes to check on the commotion he never finds anyone there. And it would certainly be odd for a party or meeting to be going on in the church without his knowing about it.

Other people have heard the sounds of this phantom party too. The castle is set far back off the road and sits alone on a hill with a large expanse of forested acreage separating it from the nearby homes. So it would be difficult to explain the party noises as coming from either a nearby house or from a loud car radio on the street below.

If the sounds do come from a ghostly party held sometime in the past it sure must have been a good one. Unlike the lost little girl in the nineteenth century dress, apparently no one wanted to go home from this party!

McCormick Mansion

In the far western suburb of Wheaton, Illinois, is a gorgeous garden of flowers and shrubbery known as Cantigny Park. Also located here is a war museum and the former mansion of the late Robert McCormick, a wealthy Chicago businessman.

The beautiful grounds belonged to the mansion when it was in active use and are bedecked with impressive stone fountains and reflecting pools as well as ornate pieces of sculpture. It was the style in which the wealthy of the early 1900s had lived. Today it is a spacious botanical park through which the public can stroll at leisure. Tours are given of the grand mansion with its wide windows, hardwood floors and plush furniture.

It doesn't seem a likely place for a haunting. It's a bright place with a bursting garden of colors and scents. But at night another mood takes over—not one of terror but more of mystery and quiet remembrance.

Buried near the corner of the mansion in an unobtrusive grave is one of the daughters of Robert McCormick. It is she who is said to haunt the great mansion. Her haunting is of the gentle variety, a simple turning on of one of the upper-story lights and an appearance briefly before the window. Maybe she loved it here so in her garden-setting home that she couldn't bear to leave it forever and comes back now and again to gaze out upon the grounds. You could understand why once you've seen Cantigny Park. The aura of the past truly lingers here.

The Wrigley Mansion

In the 1890s, William Wrigley was a struggling salesman, selling baking soda and soap. With each soap sale he gave away packages of gum as a premium to his customer. He soon discovered that the gum was much more in demand than the soap so he purchased the Zeno gum manufacturing company and started making it himself.

Thus came into being Wrigley's famous spearmint-flavored gum. It wasn't long before William Wrigley was a wealthy man and the Wrigley dynasty began. He purchased his own island off the California coast—Catalina—and a baseball team, the Chicago Cubs. Of course, he also bought Wrigley Field as well.

The Wrigley name and legacy is an institution in Chicago, even though the Cubs were sold to the *Tribune* in June of 1981. Directly across the Chicago River, just north of the loop, stands the impressive Wrigley Building, shoulder-to-shoulder with the other great landmarks towering at the water's edge.

The Wrigley mansion stands not too far north of here in a residential section of Chicago. It was built in the late nineteenth century and is constructed of heavy brownstone—a gothic-style building that seems defiant in its stance and strength. Perhaps it's because the spirit of its former owner still wanders the gloomy hallways.

The figure of the late millionaire has been seen at various places by the staff and watchman. Occasionally an upstairs light will be seen when nobody should be there. He's a hard ghost to catch sight of however. This isn't too surprising because despite his power and forcefulness, the late owner was a private man in life and apparently still is so in the afterlife.

The Stickney Mansion

Our journey takes us south from Woodstock, Illinois, to the community mentioned earlier—Crystal Lake. Crystal Lake is a town of about 22,000 people in what used to be remote McHenry County. One of the major roads in McHenry County is Cherry Valley Road and it is here that you will come upon the mysterious but well-known Stickney Mansion.

Stickney Mansion is a monumental yellow-brick building that stands out impressively from the alternately wooded and open landscape along Cherry Valley Road. The exact address is 1904 Cherry Valley Road. Since this is still a rural area the streets are dark at night and not very well marked so it would be wise to have proper directions when searching in the gloom for a haunted house. Stickney Mansion would be a perfect site to visit while en route to the haunted Woodstock Opera House since Crystal Lake is located on the same Highway 14 that continues northward to Woodstock.

The great yellow-brick mansion was built in 1894 by the eccentric millionaire, George Stickney. The ten-room box-shaped structure is architecturally peculiar in that the mansion was purposefully designed so as not to have a single right angle anywhere in the building. The idea was George Stickney's and the reason was to take away any places where spirits or demons might hide.

George Stickney and his wife were spiritualists, or at least they believed in communication with the dead. Their great mansion was the frequent site of seances and also possibly a temple for even more sinister paranormal activities. Rumors were rife about Satanic masses and witches' sabbaths on the private and secluded grounds of the wooded estate.

While the stories about demonic activity and rituals dealing with the raising of the dead were based on speculation, the holding of seances was a common and publicized occurrence. Seances were performed for several years until George Stickney shocked his friends and family by committing suicide in 1897, only three years after building his spirit-friendly mansion. For reasons still unknown he hung himself in an upstairs bedroom.

The body of George Stickney was laid out in the lavish ballroom of the mansion and was viewed by many of the notables of Chicagoland. There was also a large contingent from the psychic society to say their good-byes to his mortal remains and some may have been anxious to get in touch with him on the other side. Maybe their benefactor would have a special message for them.

Shortly after the funeral, ghostly activity began to occur at the dark and brooding Stickney mansion. If anyone had hoped to get a message from the late George Stickney their best chances would be if they remained right where they were in the ballroom where he was waked. A shadowy manifestation has been seen creeping across the ballroom and making appearances at the wide windows. Weird noises are also reported to have been heard pouring out of the ballroom.

Ghostly manifestations have also been witnessed in the upstairs bedroom where George Stickney hung himself. Like other spirits, he too returns to locations which were for him sites of violent trauma. But for what purpose? As penance? To forewarn others what could be their outcome if they should end their lives by suicide? It would indeed be very interesting to know what explanation the spirit of an avowed spiritualist would give during a seance to explain his haunting behavior.

However, George Stickney does not seem to be alone in the mansion or on the estate itself. Other manifestations have been reported—ghostly noises, phantom apparitions, and unnerving presences. Animals show a marked aversion for the Stickney property and when approaching the mansion they often show signs of extreme agitation. The grounds around the mansion are also subject to unearthly phenomena. When walking down the sidewalk alongside the great house one has the sensation that there is someone there—just out of sight. The entire grounds of the Stickney Estate are electric with this feeling. Because of the Stickney Mansion's reputation, the house and grounds have continued to be used for paranormal activities after the estate had passed to other hands. This has probably attracted even more spirits to the already haunted location. The air is charged with paranormal activity and it seems to act as a magnet to attract even more.

But let's not forget the founder and the original ghost— George Stickney. His spirit is still in the mansion; he is still the ghostly patriarch of the house. If you should drive by the estate it might behoove you to at least nod your respects to the reigning ghost of the Stickney mansion. You never know but that you might see him nod back at you.

Luetgert House

The Luetgert House is another famous dark and brooding haunted mansion located inside the city limits of Chicago. One of its locations was the corner of Hermitage and Diversey. The mansion was actually moved a couple of times before finally ending up in almost the same spot from which it was first transported. This is just one of many very unusual features concerning this very haunted building.

Adolph Luetgert had the mansion built for him in the 1890s, a time when many great mansions were being constructed all throughout Chicagoland. Luetgert was a wealthy capitalist like Philip Wrigley and Marshall Field. Instead of chewing gum or department stores, however, Luetgert was a sausage man, owning at that time the largest sausage factory in Chicago.

Adolph was married to a woman named Louise who mysteriously disappeared on May 1, 1897. Foul play was suspected and many people thought that Adolph had been the perpetrator. Not long after Louise's disappearance her wedding ring was discovered—at the bottom of a potash vat in the basement of the Luetgert sausage factory. Also found with the wedding ring were human remains.

Adolph Luetgert was charged with boiling his wife in the potash vat and then incinerating her bones in the furnace. The commonly held belief on the streets of Chicago was that Adolph had ground up Louise into sausage which, by the way, was a belief that caused sausage sales to plummet for the rest of the year. Adolph pleaded innocent to the charges of murdering his wife.

A sensational trial was held, Adolph Leutgert was found guilty of murdering Louise and he was sentenced to life imprisonment in Joliet State Penitentiary. While an inmate at Joliet, Adolph complained that the ghost of his wife was haunting him in his cell. No one else seems to have seen the ghost of Louise, but she was real enough to Adolph. One can imagine how horrifying it must have been to be haunted by an unfriendly spirit while incarcerated in a cell, unable to escape. It would certainly seem to be a just revenge for a spirit who had met such a hideous merciless death.

Adolph Luetgert died after serving only two years of his sentence. A person has to wonder if the haunting by his wife's ghost in any way hastened Adolph's end. Now that Adolph was dead, the ghost of Louise Luetgert departed from Joliet Prison and returned to its former home in Chicago. Apparently one of her favorite places in the gloomy house was by the mantelpiece in the main room because it is here that her ghost has been seen by many witnesses. She is a white-clad figure who silently leans against the mantelpiece, lost in her daydreams.

Now something quite extraordinary happened. The new owner of the Luetgert Mansion was so annoyed by the constant visits of Louise's ghost that he had the entire house physically removed for the sole purpose of escaping the ghost. The building wasn't moved far, but at its new location on Marshfield Avenue it seemed to have found a haven from the persistent spirit.

Louise's determined ghost was then spotted in the sausage factory where her death was believed to have occurred. Night watchmen reported her presence on a number of occasions in the basement near the potash vat and incinerator. Her hauntings of this location ceased only after the sausage factory mysteriously burned to the ground in 1902.

Louise's spirit moved again, this time back to the Luetgert Mansion at its new location on Marshfield Avenue. Once again the new owner of the house sought to escape the bothersome spirit by moving the house a second time. He transported it to almost the same location where it had originally stood at Diversey and Hermitage. Why he didn't choose an entirely new spot for the house is not known. Either he was trying to trick the ghost or maybe he had made some type of a bargain with the spirit of Louise Luetgert. Although the ghost still does appear in the house, it does so on a very limited basis, materializing only on the anniversaries of Louise's disappearance from earth, the first of May.

There haven't been any reports of Mr. Luetgert's ghost being seen. It's doubtful that his spirit would want to appear anywhere in the vicinity of Louise's. Ghosts have long memories.

Glessner House

The Glessner House is one of those famous dark and brooding mansions built in the late nineteenth century by the famous architect Henry Hobson Richardson and is located on South Prairie Street. The architect was so deeply involved with the construction of this building that he even managed to apparently stave off the time of his death until its completion. The famous architect died at the moment the last stone was being put in place in 1886. Many people will tell you that he is still there today, wandering the halls and admiring his creation.

Highland Park Haunted House

The suburb of Highland Park, Illinois, is north of Chicago and can be reached by following Highway 94 to Lake/Cook Road. Here amidst the affluent homes you can view a twenty-eight-room mansion that was owned by a film producer in the late 1940s and early 1950s. A tragic story was played out here when the already-married film producer killed himself over a hopeless affair with a younger woman. Shortly thereafter, his romantic interest also killed herself. The great mansion is haunted by the spirit of the film producer as well as by the spirit of his ill-fated lover. It seems that in the afterlife they have found a ghostly type of union.

WATERY GRAVES

Old Bill's Warning

The following is a very obscure little-known story. Not many people associate Chicago with waterway ghosts. This particular account was found in the *Chicago Times* newspaper of March 1885.

Chicago is a major hub of transportation due to its railway system and major airport, but few people take into account the waterway traffic that this great city handles. In the nineteenth century Lake Michigan was an extremely important link to the east via the other Great Lakes and the rivers that fed off of them. Chicago was home to many great harbors and ports and was the base for many commercial shipping companies.

On one occasion one of these lake schooners was preparing to deliver cargo to Buffalo. The stores were being hauled aboard and the crew was busy getting the ship ready for sailing. Two of the men were high overhead working on the topmast of the schooner. Then, without warning and for no apparent cause, the men lost their holds on the topmast and plunged to the deck below. Both were killed instantly.

Despite the tragedy, the ship left Chicago and sailed as scheduled to Buffalo. But once there the entire crew deserted because they believed that the deaths of the two men had made her an unlucky ship and no one wanted to sail on her. The captain of the ship had a hard time even getting men to unload the cargo as word of the ship's ill-omened nature quickly spread. The captain finally managed to get the ship unloaded and its new cargo brought aboard.

The captain at last got a crew to sail her but as they prepared to set sail one of the mates noticed something very odd on the schooner's topmast. It looked like a figurehead. Why would any ship have a figurehead jutting out from its topmast? When the mate pointed this out to the other crew members, he was

P. Reed

told it was 'Old Bill,' one of the two men who had been killed in the fall from the topmast. It was his ghost. Did he come back as a warning?

At the sight of Old Bill's ghost the crew that the captain had worked so hard to get fled the unlucky ship. That left the captain with the task of going out and scrounging up another crew, which he somehow did. This crew remained aboard the ship—apparently not being paid a visit by Old Bill's ghost—and set sail for Cleveland from which they were then to return to port in Chicago. The schooner never reached Cleveland, however. The unlucky ship collided with another schooner and sank. One wonders why Old Bill didn't warn this crew of the impending disaster. Could it be that they were fated to be the unlucky ones to go down with the ship?

Duchess III

Our journey into the world of ghosts once again crosses the path of Mr. Alphonse Capone. He has left many ghosts in his wake, some on land and some on sea. Wherever Al went he also took his penchant for violence and explosive temper, even while sailing.

Al Capone was a sportsman and renowned fisherman who owned a number of yachts in his time. One of them he named the *Duchess III* after one of his favorite prostitutes. No one could ever accuse Mr. Capone of being a social snob.

The *Duchess III* had a lot of use over a ten-year period, not all of which was for simple pleasure fishing and island hopping, although Al did a lot of that too. He had to escape somehow from his busy schedule of assassinations and gangland hits.

In fairness to Mr. Capone, however, it should be noted that he purchased the *Duchess III* secondhand and its original owner was far from being an exemplary citizen, engaging in gun running and various bloody crimes of his own. Thus, not all of the ghosts on this haunted yacht may necessarily be attributed to the Capone period of ownership. But, knowing Al, it's hard to imagine that he didn't contribute his fair share of ghosts to this boat.

The once-elegant yacht had fallen into great disrepair in the years after Capone's ownership and it was during the process of restoration that the numerous phantoms aboard were raised from the dark again. In the bow of the boat below decks is the so-called "ghost room" due to the recurrent apparitions that occur here. Among these are the moaning of a woman and the crying of a baby. According to psychics these cries originate from a woman who had given birth aboard the ship. The figure of a man has been seen tearing the baby from her arms and tossing it into the water. Then he grabs the woman and consigns her to the same fate. No one is sure whether the deed was done by Capone or not.

The tragic scene apparently can be viewed and clearly heard by dogs. The German shepherd of one of the new owners, when taken aboard the ship, raced toward one of the port holes, shoved his head through the opening and howled with uncommon ferocity even for him. There was nobody below decks at the time, yet the dog certainly was reacting to something quite horrifying.

Another very common occurrence in the "ghost room" is an intense cold zone. When one of the new owners was refurbishing the "ghost room" he was suddenly overwhelmed by a frigid mass of air which refused to dissipate. He rushed up onto the deck where the temperature hovered near ninety degrees. This same phenomenon also occurred to a real estate agent who had come aboard to view the boat. She was suddenly surrounded by a cold mass of air which twined itself about her and passed what she felt to be icy fingers through her hair. She quickly fled the area.

Strange lights are another very common manifestation on the *Duchess III*. Fishermen ashore have noticed a light like that of a candle passing from port hole to port hole down the entire length of the ship. Two things make this very odd. First, no one should've been aboard the *Duchess III* at that time and second, if someone was walking around with a candle he couldn't have passed from one end of the ship to the other in the manner described because a wall separates the yacht in the middle. This mysterious light has been seen by other people as well. A man who was painting the hull of the boat also saw the candlelight pass along the length of the yacht from port hole to port hole while no one was aboard the ship.

Candlelight seems to have a particular fascination for the ghost or ghosts which haunt this ship. Annoyed by the ghostly activity, one person asked the spirits to give some type of evidence as to their presence aboard ship. At that point, two of the candles in a candelabra flared very noticeably. Not convinced, the person requested to see that same act done again. And it was! Does this represent some type of communication with a disembodied spirit or merely an oddly well-timed draft sweeping about the ship, causing only two candles to flare up out of the five available?

Who haunts the *Duchess III*? No one knows for sure. One of the ghosts could even belong to Al Capone. While alive, Mr. Capone made the Hawthorne Inn on 22nd Street in Cicero his favorite haunt. He took over the entire hotel, had bulletproof shutters and electronically-controlled doors installed, and placed armed thugs at all the entrances. Apparently, Al thought that somebody might be out to get him. Ironically, no one ever did get Al and he died peacefully at his Florida retreat.

But how many ghosts did he leave behind at the Hawthorne Inn? It was from here that he and his business associates notables like Greasy Thumb Guzick, Machine Gun McGurn and John Scalisi—held their Board of Directors meetings which often involved assassination plots on rival business owners. Sometimes, even the members of Capone's own Board of Directors were killed by their boss during one of their meetings like on the occasion when Capone battered to death John Scalisi, Joseph Galena, and Albert Anselmi with a baseball bat.

While these potentially murderous business meetings were transpiring in Al Capone's office, vice went on as normal throughout the rest of the hotel. Prostitutes busily tended to their clients, bookies diligently placed bets on upcoming races, and booze was freely served on tap to the local patrons.

Al Capone has been covered a great deal in this book not only because of the many ghosts that seem to surround his life and death but also because he is a product of Chicagoland and one of its most representative characters. He was a flashy brutal entrepreneur who gave the people exactly what they wanted, and a hero to many. He was never convicted of any violent crime but was finally jailed for not paying income taxes. He probably also voted early and voted often in that good old Chicago tradition.

WHO YOU GONNA CALL?

The Witch's Knock

Follow Highway 55 back north to Joliet again for this next case of haunting. I've changed the name of the person who is the subject of this story to Mary Maple.

Seldom does a person come across a haunted house that truly looks like what a haunted house is generally depicted as looking like—a symmetrically-shaped structure at the end of a road which has been deserted for a long time but which still has some of the furnishings left in it. This is what the elderly Mrs. Maple's house looked like, a house in which Mrs. Maple had lived—and died—by herself. She suffered some type of medically-produced attack, dragged herself across the floor to the front door where she died while knocking for help.

The knocking noise made by a witch's spirit rang through this small neighborhood one summer day in the late 1960s. (Author's photo.)

Mrs. Maple was a recluse who had a reputation of being a witch. Her house was practically buried beneath deep dark foliage and could barely be seen even on the brightest of days. Many of the plants that grew on her property, which was in the shape of an isosceles triangle that came to an extreme point near a prison graveyard, were extraordinary botanical specimens. There were trees with thick rope-like vines, shooting bushes which spewed oversized seeds from their pods, and herbs and flowers of mysterious nature. Nowhere else in this part of

The yard of exotic trees and herbs belonging to the woman whose spirit caused the witch's knock. (Author's photo.)

the state had I seen foliage like this outside of a botanical garden—just the type of plants a witch would use for her brews. There was even a working, old-fashioned well in the back yard for pumping pure ground water.

No one knew of Mrs. Maple's death for several days. When she was finally discovered she was whisked away with such speed and secrecy that it was as if she'd been taken by the Devil Himself. This naturally added to her legend of being a witch.

Mrs. Maple's house was very near my own boyhood home. Her empty brooding house stood there for years, silent and untouched, slowly overgrown by the foliage now gone wild. Nothing really unusual happened there—no ghostly sightings or noises—until one humid, overcast summer day long after the woman had died. The air was heavy and very still, the kind of air that conducts sound very well. There wasn't any wind or any loud noises from construction or any other type of clamor.

Then the air was suddenly filled by a loud unearthly rapping. It sounded louder than any sound should be, as if it were somehow amplified. I was alone and standing about three hundred feet from Mrs. Maple's house when the loud repetitious knocking occurred and I could verify that it was coming from it. My first thought was that someone was inside the house and was banging on the wooden floorboards. So I hurried to the house, fighting through the clinging vegetation only to find that no one was there or had been there. I would have heard and or seen anyone running from the property.

By this time, the brief series of knocks had ceased and I left the deserted house, crossing that very same threshold on which Mrs. Maple had died. I was standing in my own yard pondering whether anyone else had heard this strange sound when a friend from a neighborhood about a mile away came to visit my brother. The first words out of his mouth were to ask me if we were building something over here because of the loud rapping sound he'd heard. The neighbor, who had later gone into the construction business, had come over to see if he could help us with whatever we were building. I told him about the mysterious rapping to which he knowingly nodded and then continued on up the front steps of my porch.

This unusual knocking was the only ghostly manifestation that I've ever known to come from Mrs. Maple's house. Could it have been the sound of her knocking on her door for help during the last moments of her mortal life? If so, this time someone heard it. Unfortunately, it was too late to help her unless she'd been calling for someone to pray for her restless soul.

Dark Intruders

Almost directly west of Wheaton, Illinois off of Roosevelt Road or Highway 38 is West Chicago. On an normal street in this small suburban town lives an average family of a mother and her two young daughters. The two visitors to their home, however, are not at all average. I would classify them as specters or unfriendly ghosts. Since this is a recent story I have chosen not to divulge the names of those involved or the location of their home.

It all started one day when the youngest daughter felt someone or something tugging at the bottom of her dress. When she turned to see who it could be she was startled by the sight of a haggish-looking woman dressed in a ragged clothing and who seemed to be extending outward from one of the window curtains. Breaking free, the little girl wasted no time rushing downstairs to her mother. Skeptical at first, the mother agreed to go upstairs to check on the situation. When she entered her daughter's bedroom she didn't see anything out of the ordinary but noted that it felt rather cooler than normal there. Nothing more to be done, she quieted her daughter and assured her that everything was all right.

But everything wasn't all right. Sometime later, the little girl was awakened from her sleep by the same spectral woman, this time tugging at her bed covers. Screaming, the girl bolted from bed and raced into her mother's room, refusing to leave the safety of her mother's bed that night. Her older sister, somehow having slept through the commotion, remained in the upper berth of the bunk bed.

It wasn't long after this that the older daughter was herself startled by a strange apparition. While leaving her bedroom one day she was surprised to see a dark figure lurking behind her door. She too hurried to her mother with a frantic story of a weird creature in their house.

Things became steadily worse. The frightening entities began to appear more regularly, and sometimes together. On one occasion the older daughter noted that the dark hideous figure that she'd first seen lurking outside the door was now standing behind the old crone who was besetting her sister. The two spirits appeared to be partners in this haunting.

Realizing the gravity of the problem now, the mother sought the help of a researcher in the paranormal. The researcher, together with a psychic, discovered that there were indeed a pair of sinister forces roaming the house. Their suggestion was an exorcism, which was duly performed. In conjunction with this, the mother hung tiny bells from locations at the heads of the two girls' beds which they were to ring in order to scare away the troubling spectres.

The exorcism and the bell ringing strategy has apparently been successful but there is still an uneasy calm in the air of this seemingly average American home. More time will have to pass in order to be sure if the unwanted spirits have truly been rung from the house for good.

Poltergeist Rampage

I'm going to take a slight detour from our strictly Chicagoland ghost search to investigate a poltergeist story of fantastic scope. While it made its first noted American debut in the town of Kokomo, Indiana, it also visited Chicagoland.

The astounding poltergeist episode began in England in early May 1952. A teenage girl was driving down a road in the county of Lincolnshire when suddenly her windshield was shattered by an unknown force. At the time it didn't seem like anything more than a simple broken windshield.

But as it was to turn out it was not just a simple matter of a rock or other piece of debris striking her windshield causing it to shatter. A few days later, on the same road, the windshield of a truck was similarly shattered and the following day the windshield of a school bus full of children was demolished as well. Yet another driver's windshield was smashed on a road a few miles north of where the others were shattered.

Was there someone firing some type of pellet into the windshields of these unsuspecting drivers? If so, why was no missile or projectile ever found at any of the scenes of window breakage? Surely there would have been some physical evidence.

The windshield shatterings continued. On June 12 there were several incidents near the town of Newbury. In one instance, whoever or whatever the culprit was missed the windshields of its intended targets and struck the side of the vehicle instead. But just as before there was no physical evidence to show what had caused the tiny holes that had been bored into the metal sides of the vehicles.

The authorities had no idea what had caused the rash of over one hundred windshield shatterings but they attempted an explanation anyway. They theorized that the breakage had been caused by either unusual stress on the glass, distortions of the frame the glass was in, vibrations from the road surface, extreme changes of temperature, or sound waves. This sounds almost convincing except for the fact that this type of windshield breakage had not occurred before and did not take in account why so many happened all at the same time. And then, just as suddenly as the phenomena had started, it stopped. At least in England.

On September 22, 1952, over fifty business owners in Kokomo, Indiana, went into their shops to find that tiny holes had been pierced through their plate glass store windows. The police were called and, upon investigation, ballistic experts discovered that all of the holes were smaller than the size of a common BB shot or any other gun of a like kind and that the punctures had all come from the inside. Not even in one single case was there any evidence left behind as to what type of missile had caused the damage. Likewise, there was not even the hint of a vandal who might have been the culprit.

Captain Unger ordered tests to be made with every type of weapon that could possibly make the type of holes that were found in the Kokomo plate glass store windows. The results were definitive: there was no such weapon!

The window breaking continued and spread over the entire business district. A plea was put out by the local newspaper, the *Kokomo Tribune*, asking anyone with any information on this matter to come forward. No one did.

The force that was causing the vandalism took an excursion up the road to Peru, Indiana where it also engaged in its favorite sport. However, there it broke only a handful of windows before returning to Kokomo where it engaged in another round of window smashing before abruptly stopping for two years.

Then in April 1954 the force reappeared in Bellingham, Washington with a vengeance. Over 1,500 windshields were mysteriously damaged over a week's time. Storefront windows also were broken. And just as before, there was no physical evidence of a missile or any other projectile that could have caused the damage. So fierce was the glass-battering in Bellingham that *LIFE Magazine*—from which some of my information is taken—wrote a story on it in its April 12, 1954 edition.

Seattle was next in line for attack. The force broke hundreds of windows there in one night, gaining press in that city's major newspaper as well. The police chief was furious and exasperated. There wasn't the hint of a culprit to be found or any other evidence. It was simply something that could not be fought or stopped.

Glass-breaking attacks even occurred across the border in Canada. One witness, Mrs. May, stuck her hand out of her car window while the windshield was in the process of being pelted. She was struck by something that stung and made her flesh burn. Another person had a similar experience.

Then on April 17, 1954, the force made a coast-to-coast foray, attacking from Los Angeles to New England to

This truck window in Bellingham, Washington was hit while the driver was at the wheel. (*Life*, April 12, 1954)

Cleveland to Chicago. Chicago was hard hit and was one of the last locations where the window breaking occurred. After April 17, 1954 there were no more reports of this particular window-shattering force. It seemed to have spent all of its energy on its last destructive binge and faded into nothingness after tearing through Chicago.

How can such an astonishing phenomenon be accounted for? One explanation points to a poltergeist. Poltergeists are known for their awesome destructive force and for the frivolous nature of their outpourings of energy. They're like a demigod throwing a temper tantrum.

There are many specific similarities between poltergeist activities and the window-breaking force that spanned two years and two continents. As already noted, one similarity would be the force of energy used and the frivolous manner in which it was directed. Although a lot of damage was done, no serious injury was incurred by anyone other than the mild burning of the skin by some unnaturally-heated elements as is common in poltergeist events.

Another similarity between the two is the abrupt starting and stopping of the event and the long time lapse in between any recurrence of the same manifestation. Poltergeist attacks begin and end suddenly and if they resume often do so after a lengthy period of time has passed.

If the force that had caused the thousands of window breakings had not been of a poltergeist-like nature, what can account for such widespread, senseless, unstoppable destruction? One possibility that comes to mind is that of atomic fallout. Between the years of 1952 and 1954 a great deal of experimentation was being done with atomic bombs, both in laboratories and in atmospheric tests. Could the invisible missiles that struck the thousands of destroyed windshields

Some car owners tried to protect their windshields from the mysterious force with newspapers, cardboard and other materials. (*Life*, April 12, 1954)

and windows have been some form of nuclear fallout which acted on the glass by burning into it, causing it to explode?

Since we've delved into the realm of physics there is another scientific possibility that might explain the amazing window breakings. Could the damage have been caused by antimatter? Is it possible that these episodic periods of glass-attacks were caused by the earth passing through a wayward stream of these matter-hating particles? If so, however, why would windows and windshields be the only targets?

There aren't any official answers to the window-breaking outbreak between 1952 and 1954. This doesn't mean an answer doesn't exist, just that it hasn't been found yet. In the meantime, keep a close eye on your windows and your neighbor's windows; you never know when the gods might throw another tantrum!

Rest Haven

Rest Haven Park sounds like it would be a nice quiet place to live. But all it takes is one annoying poltergeist to ruin everyone's peace or, in this particular case, provide some entertainment during the dog days of summer. Rest Haven is located in Preston Heights, a small community just south of Joliet, Illinois. It is here that another noteworthy case of poltergeist infestation occurred during August 1957.

It started innocently enough as most such cases do with simple things like tape measures falling off the table and onto the floor by themselves. But enough of these minor incidents took place to warrant calling the local sheriff's department to ask for an investigation although usually a priest or minister is considered a more likely person to deal with such events.

On arriving at the residence of Mr. and Mrs. James Mikulecky, Deputy Sheriff Chester Moberly was faced with a situation he couldn't control. The family, who lived here with their thirteen-year-old granddaughter, reported hearing strange rappings and soundings. The granddaughter had been subjected to violent bed-shakings and there were peculiar whistling sounds coming from nowhere. The most visible and startling demonstration was when a group of pencils rose up and scudded purposefully across the top of a table and clattered onto the floor.

The sheriff's department was frustrated and could do nothing to help the besieged family. The Mikuleckys had been enduring these inconveniences for about a month and decided that their best course of action would be to get out of their home. Fortunately, they had a sympathetic neighbor nearby who let the Mikuleckys move in with them for a time.

But it wasn't long before the same ghostly events that had occurred in the Mikulecky's home began to manifest themselves in their neighbor's home as well. The poltergeist had followed them. However, it wasn't long after this that the poltergeist activity began to die down as abruptly as it had started. But it is important to note that it had continued for a short time after the Mikuleckys had moved in with their neighbors. This greatly reduces the possibility of fraud or deception. While it was possible for someone to produce the ghostly effects in the well-known environment of their own home, it would have been extremely difficult for them to continue to have done so in an unfamiliar and controlled environment. Furthermore, it's not uncommon for poltergeists to follow their victims.

The poltergeist affair had been quite an amazing event in the Mikulecky's neighborhood, almost a sideshow providing entertainment during the slow days of summer. The loud noises and rappings would be heard coming from the poltergeist home and the neighbors would crowd the streets, watching and waiting for whatever might happen next. There was no shortage of witnesses and coverage by the local newspaper was relentless.

The sheriff's department decided that there was nothing worth investigating and retired from the scene. They were helpless against these strange forces anyway and couldn't be blamed for not knowing how to deal with them. There was no one they could grab and handcuff to stop the strange occurrences and since the manifestations had been harmless and provided a type of entertainment, the police weren't eager to attempt forced intervention.

The Rest Haven incident was a classic poltergeist case in which the disturbances seem to have been generated either by extreme stress or by the natural psychic energies of a pre-pubescent child who is at the center of it all. The phenomenon seemed to be under the control of the Mikulecky's granddaughter.

Then there is what appears to be the second cousin to the Mikulecky case, which is an elemental form of poltergeist whose center of consciousness may be a disincarnate being of nonhuman form. These manifestations usually demonstrate a violent dangerousness as opposed to the more capricious, even playful, poltergeist.

A Tame Spirit

Travelling to the northwestern suburbs of Chicago, we find our next haunting in the community of Des Plaines, Illinois, which is reached by taking Highway 90 west. What we find here is a completely different type of poltergeist. Not only is it a harmless spirit, but it is even benevolent.

Once again, because this is a current story I am not divulging the exact location of the haunting or the real names of the people involved. The house was purchased over twenty years ago by Grace and Harry Wingate. From the moment that they took possession they knew that there was something odd about the place.

The Wingate's home is a very ordinary two-story structure on a very typical suburban street. But the spirit or spirits that had remained inside the structure were most unusual. Because the most pronounced manifestations involve the actual physical movement of objects the spirit is likely to be a poltergeist. The phenomena has been taking place since the house was purchased and still continues. The manifestations are very basic, very simple, and more amusing than scary. They involve the moving of objects and hiding them, then returning them after a passage of time—almost like the type of game a child might play.

Although the Wingates have three children—all of whom are now grown—they could not be linked to the paranormal activity. This in itself is highly unusual in poltergeist cases because a preadolescent child is usually at the center of the activity. But the Wingate's children were much too young to have performed the disappearing tricks.

For instance, there was the case of the disappearing trivet, a three-legged stand for holding kettles or pots. The trivet disappeared from the kitchen one day and was not seen again until about a year later. When it did reappear it was found at the bottom of the basement stairs. Mr. Wingate noted that it would be asking too much of his toddler children to have taken the trivet, hidden it for such a long period of time, and then brought it out from hiding. After all, a child's patience can be calculated in minutes not months. For another, it's doubtful that a child could remember where he'd hidden something almost a year ago. Even if all of this could be accomplished by the brightest and most precocious of kids it wouldn't seem that there would be much reward in it for him. But poltergeists sure like to play this type of trick!

Another of the phenomena experienced at the Wingate house is the sound of pacing footsteps in the upstairs hallway when no one is there. The sound has occurred at times when the two younger children were napping downstairs and the older son was out of the house.

Mrs. Wingate believes that the footsteps belong to the previous owner of the house. Because of this belief she no longer fears the unusual sounds that occur nor the sudden disappearances of household objects. She regards the spirit more as a friend and a guardian rather than an unwanted intruder. It certainly appears that this pleasant, though sometimes mischievous spirit, regards her with the same esteem.

Flaming Curtains

Poltergeists are usually of a destructive nature unlike the one in Des Plaines. They are often incendiary creatures: they like to set things on fire. The famous ghost hunter Harry Price once witnessed in his youth the fiery wrath of a poltergeist.

In Brockley, England there was a house that was well-known because once a week the owner refinished the front steps with red-ochre paint. But it was the always dingy-looking yellow curtains that gave the house its reputation of being unfashionable.

The house on Shardeloes Road was owned by a retired Norwegian navy man named Petersen. He lived there with his wife and employed a young girl as a servant. The servant girl later proved to be the instigator of what happen there.

The young Harry Price was coming home from a nearby playground when he passed the house with the faded yellow curtains. A large noisy crowd was standing around the house and Harry joined it to see what was happening. What he saw was that every window that had once sported the long conspicuous yellow curtains was now bare of them and that the venetian blind that covered the drawing-room window on the lower floor was on fire.

In the space of ten minutes the ten sets of curtains had simultaneously caught fire and disintegrated in flames throughout the large house. Only minor scorching had occurred to the poles on which the curtains had been hung. The venetian blind had caught fire from a lingering spark. Just the curtains had burned!

Presumably the fire was started by the mental and emotional machinations of the youthful servant girl who set her poltergeist force out to denude the house of those awful yellow curtains—a case in which a poltergeist doubled as an interior decorator?

It is only by studying cases such as these that a person can make some sense out what happened to a family in Chicago in

1892. The family had been away from town on a lengthy trip and when they returned they were shocked to find that every lace curtain in their home had been yanked from its window and stomped on with great vigor. Drawers throughout the house had been torn open and ransacked but nothing was taken. Apparently whoever or whatever had gone through the drawers was searching for more curtains. Another odd feature about this event is that when the curtain-yanking and drawer-tugging occurred there were no humans on the premises. So, if a poltergeist is to blame, it had to have performed its act over a long distance.

The police were called to investigate but they were completely baffled. Not only couldn't they find any clues as to who or what the culprits might have been but they couldn't even explain how entrance to the still tightly-locked house had been affected.

At any rate, if you ever plan on hanging fashionably questionable curtains you might want to consider who else may be watching other than just your neighbors.

SPOOKY LORE...
NOTHING MORE?

Coal Mine Tragedy
Apparitions From Below

Coal City is a small town of several thousand people south of Joliet, Illinois, and is on the extreme southern border of Chicagoland. As its name implies, it is a city which owes its existence to the coal mining industry that was so prevalent here in the early part of the twentieth century. Chicago was a major consumer of coal and was easily accessed either by river or railway.

Towns like Coal City and Carbon Hill were large enough and had a diverse enough economy to survive the end of coal era. Other towns in the region weren't so fortunate and are now ghost towns in their own right. Torino is one of these former communities, named after a city in Italy by its predominantly Italian citizenry. Another of the ghost towns is Godly, the origin of whose name upon which I choose not to speculate. All that remains of Torino and Godly are a few stones lying amidst the tangle of underbrush.

Coal City has survived and is a pleasant community set in the quiet countryside. Its coal mining heritage is kept alive in the schoolrooms and in the local library where books on the era and artifacts from those bygone days are preserved for all to study. This special heritage is kept alive in a truly spiritual way as well.

As in all coal mining communities the potential for disaster was ever present. Coal City was no different. One day the event that everyone dreaded occurred. The alarm whistle went off, signalling a cave in at one of the mines. Townspeople rushed to the site of the disaster, medical teams flew to the area, and the local newspaper diligently covered the story.

Unfortunately, the outcome was tragic. Several of the miners were killed in the cave in, buried alive underground. There was nothing more for the grieving people to do but return to their homes and lament the dead.

Years passed, the mine where the disaster had occurred was closed, plowed over, and turned over to real estate developers. In time, houses were built over the site. One of my in-laws lived in one these homes and it is from her that this account is taken.

Her home was an ordinary home like any other in the town. It was on a quiet tree-lined street in an ordinary neighborhood. But some of the visitors to this particular house were far from ordinary.

Her house was built directly over the mine shaft where the disastrous cave in had occurred. On many occasions the occupants of the house would be sitting peacefully in the living room and have their quiet afternoon or evening disturbed by a group of dust-covered miners trooping across the floor from out of nowhere. One by one they would tramp past and disappear into the wall and oblivion. Maybe in spiritual form they'll eventually find their way out of their deep tomb.

Perhaps Coal City should also be considered a ghost town like Torino and Godly due to these truly ghostly residents. It makes a person wonder how many ghosts may be roaming the overgrown fields above Torino and Godly without there being anyone to witness their passing.

The Lady of the Woods

Porter County, Indiana, is in the northeastern part of the state and not too far across the border from Illinois. It is well within the domain of Chicagoland because it is only a short drive away on Highway 80/90 east. The haunting takes place

between the two small communities of Chesterton and Liberty, Indiana, on a remote stretch known as Meridian Road.

This is a classic type of ghost story with a bizarre twist. No one knows for certain when the 'Lady of the Woods,' as she is called, made her first appearance but legends of her have apparently been around for a good many years. Her reappearance a few days after Halloween in 1965 caused a sensation among the residents of this county who had heard tales of the mournful phantom all their lives. Something like a stampede was set loose when word of her sighting got out.

The long, dark road that runs through a dense wood between Chesterton and Liberty is usually a quiet, deserted place. It is on this remote, secluded tract that the apparition occurs. Hidden in the woods that fringe Meridian Road is a gloomy pond and an even less inviting swamp which is where the Lady of the Woods met her death with her baby—whether by accident or foul play is uncertain.

A faceless woman dressed in white arises from the darkness and with child in arms flickers through the woods wailing, "Save my baby!" People driving by have been startled by the terrifying sight and when they've slowed down either to help or get a closer look, the apparition approaches the car, still sobbing, and scratches on the window with her free hand.

Reports of the Lady of the Woods sightings in 1965 drew an unprecedented reaction. The once lonely infrequently-used road between Chesterton and Liberty was now heavy with traffic. Many of the more adventurous ghost hunters detoured from the road into the nearby fields in search of the ghost and her baby, some of them with headlights doused so as not to annoy the apparition. At least one of the farmers whose land was being trampled didn't mind too much; he was charging a one dollar parking fee.

One group of lucky sightseers caught a glimpse of the Lady of the Woods without having to leave their car. A swirling white form floating amongst the trees came directly toward them crying, "Save me! Save my baby!"

Other people came to the site with intentions other than just sight-seeing. For them, 'ghost hunting' meant exactly that—getting out whatever weapon you had handy and tracking down the apparition to "kill it." Suddenly, a ghost hunting frenzy developed. Dozens of people came to scour the dark fields armed with shotguns, hunting knives, and revolvers—one person even brought a tracking dog—for the purpose of shooting the ghost! The situation got out of control and had to be ended by forceful action of the sheriff's department. Many arrests were made and after several days the ghost hunting was brought to a halt and all was quiet again on Meridian Road.

A daytime visit to the haunted site could be well worth the effort. However, a nighttime visit is discouraged because it is a dangerous location in full daylight, requiring a person to have a good acquaintance with the terrain. The woods are dense and overgrown with heavy underbrush and in the midst of the forest is treacherous swamp. It is dark, dank and foreboding here—just the right place to find a faceless wailing ghost.

Maybe the best explanation for the ghost is the inhospitable terrain itself. A woman out here alone with a baby would be in a desperate condition under any circumstances. Does the ghost of the Lady of the Woods belong to a woman of long ago who, by some violent misfortune, had been deserted in the wilderness with her child? Or had she somehow become lost in these dreary woods, meeting her death by drowning in the swamp?

Perhaps a major clue to the identity of the Lady of the Woods is that she lacks a face. Does this represent a supernatural marking of guilt for some heinous deed that she might of committed—maybe against her own baby?

None of these questions can be answered until physical evidence or other documentation is discovered. Until then, the Lady of the Woods will continue her wandering along dark and secluded Meridian Road, wailing for someone to help save her baby. But save it from whom?

Until Death Do Us Shop
Mail Order Giants, Sears and Ward

It seems that Richard Warren Sears and Aaron Montgomery Ward were destined not only to lead similar and competitive lives but to continue this type of relationship even into the afterlife. Both men were giants of merchandising in Chicago. Both men were innovators in the area of mail-order marketing and both built vast empires. Both men are buried in Rosehill Cemetery in Chicago.

Aaron Montgomery Ward

Aaron Montgomery Ward began his life in merchandising as a salesman for $6.00 a month and room and board in a general store in St. Joseph, Michigan. Sensing the anger of the farmers over profits made by the middle-men, he conceived of the idea of buying products at wholesale prices then selling them cheaply. It was Aaron Ward who produced the first mail-order catalogue in August 1872, using only $1,600 for the project. The catalogue was only a single sheet of paper but it listed over one hundred fifty items that could be purchased at greatly discounted prices. Ward also introduced the concept of the money-back guarantee in his 1875 catalogue.

By 1888, Ward's annual sales were a staggering $1,000,000 and at his death in 1913 they had risen to $40,000,000. In 1886, Ward turned over operations of his company to his brother-in-law, George R. Thorne, who had bought a half interest in the company in 1873 for a mere five hundred dollars. Ward remained president of the company but devoted most of his time to preserving the natural resources of the Chicago lake front. However, despite his great successes he was never able to displace the name of Sears as the most popular merchandising company in America.

Richard Warren Sears was born December 7, 1863 in Stewartville, Minnesota. Although his father had been a wealthy man, he lost his fortune through bad speculation and Richard was forced to find work. He got a job with the railway and wound up purchasing a shipment of watches that had been rejected by a Redwood Falls jeweler. Sears turned around and sold the watches to railroad station managers at a reduced price and made a profit of $5,000. He started a mail-order watch business with that money in 1886, calling it the R. W. Sears Watch Company.

Before the year was out, Sears moved his business to Chicago and hired Alvah Roebuck as a watch repairman. Another mail order catalogue was put out and made another large profit. Sears then sold his business for $100,000 and moved to Iowa. He soon became bored with life as a mere banker in Iowa and then started another mail-order firm, selling watches and jewelry again, this time in partnership with Alvah Roebuck. This is the company that became the famous Sears, Roebuck and Company in Chicago in 1893.

The Sears, Roebuck catalogue grew to vast dimensions, offering just about anything a person could want. Almost all of the design and copy for the catalogue of over five hundred pages was done by Richard Sears. In 1895, Roebuck sold his interest in the company to Julius Rosenwald, a wealthy clothing manufacturer. In 1909, Richard Sears resigned as president over a dispute on the advertising budget and moved to a farm north of Chicago where he hoped to enjoy a quiet peaceful life far away from merchandising. He died on September 28, 1914 in Waukesha, Wisconsin.

The lives of Ward and Sears paralleled each other in many ways. One irony is that Sears was born on December 7 and Ward died on December 7. Taking into account all of the other similarities between these two men, this oddity of birth and death dates seems more provocative than a mere coincidence.

Sears and Ward died within a year of each other and both were buried in the exclusive Rosehill Cemetery a mere thirty feet from each other. But, just as in life, it appears that Sears is also upstaging Ward in death. While the spirit of Aaron Montgomery Ward has been little noted in the graveyard, that of Mr. Sears has made a resounding impression. The great catalogue merchandiser has been seen on many occasions strolling casually through the stately Rosehill mausoleum attired in top hat and tails. It's almost as if his illustrious spirit is master of the halls of this great building of the dead and makes frequent rounds through its domain.

A person can only guess what the spirit of Aaron Montgomery Ward must think of such goings on. Perhaps he's wondering where Sears got his top hat and tails.

R-Rated Wraiths

We return to Illinois for these two stories. They are similar to the Porter County, Indiana ghost in a couple of interesting ways.

The first ghost story is from Byron, Illinois, a little bit of a distance from Chicago. It is a very curious tale of a scantily-clad female ghost who appears to enjoy teasing witnesses in more ways than one.

Similar to the specter in Porter County, this ghost also appears along a dark stretch of road known as Kennedy Hill Road. The scantily-clad spook creates a commotion of her own, causing long lines of traffic to slowly crawl down the road in search of her whenever news of her latest sighting is heard.

Not only does she draw the attention of viewers by her lack of full attire but when someone does get close enough for a good look—she disappears. No explanation has been found as to the identity or origins of this ghost. But this doesn't seem to matter to the hundreds of thrill seekers who come out to get a glimpse of this tantalizing specter.

Another scantily-clad traffic-stopping ghost is often seen on the extreme far north side of Chicago at Oakton Street and Sheridan Road. On the west side of Sheridan Road is Calvary Cemetery and on the east side is Lake Michigan. The specter is seen to rise up from the shore of the Lake and make a mad dash across Sheridan into the cemetery, bringing traffic to a sudden halt. By its attire and appearance, the ghost is thought to be a Lake Michigan drowning victim. It's also a ghost with a very handy cemetery plot to rush to, directly across the street from where it had died. Now if it can only keep from being run down by a car . . .

Wedding Bell Blues in Naperville

From Chicago we next travel to the southwest suburbs and the city of Naperville, Illinois. Once a sleepy little farming community, Naperville, is now a large sprawling city and the home site of many nationally-known corporations. For one spirit, however, the streets of early twentieth century Naperville still exist. This is the spirit of the woman who was jilted on her wedding day and was so severely hurt that she continued to wear her wedding dress day after day as she walked the main streets of town. Her father eventually placed her in an institution where she soon died. But her spirit has returned and can be seen on certain nights walking the old main streets of Naperville still wearing her wedding gown.

The Forgetful Ghost

Apparently, not all dead people wish to be buried, nor remember their own names. The case of the unhappy bookbinder is one of the strangest I've come across. It was reported in the *Institute Quarterly* magazine which was published by the Illinois's Charity Services.

We return to the simpler days of 1916 and travel to the small town of Bartonville, Illinois. It was a time when life was slower and living wasn't as complex as it is today. But many problems of life that we have today existed back then, though often called by different names. People still grew old and some suffered from what was then called 'senility'; today we would call it Alzheimer's disease but the symptoms are the same.

In 1916, people's lives weren't nearly as regulated by the state as they are today. There were no credit cards and no social security numbers. Purchases were often made with cash and you could live your life in anonymity if you wanted. That's why it was possible for a person to die in 1916 without family or friends, without knowing his own name, and to be buried without any other identification than what his occupation had been.

The ghost of this story used to work as a bookbinder. He'd outlived the company that he'd worked for and apparently all its other employees. When he died in the 'old folks home' the only thing that anyone knew about him was that he used to work as a bookbinder for that company that went out of business a long time ago. He had forgotten his own name before even having been brought to the home and couldn't remember the names of any existing family, if there was any.

When it came time for his burial he was bestowed the identity of A. Bookbinder because of his former profession. The horse-drawn hearse conveyed the coffin to the old town cemetery followed by a great many of the residents of the home. The plain wooden coffin was transported to the grave site, a brief service was said, then the casket was slowly lowered into the ground.

The mourners were just turning to depart when all of sudden there was a commotion at the plot. The dead man's coffin flew out of the grave before it could be fully lowered and landed precariously on the dirt mound at the edge of the plot! Startled witnesses watched as the dead man's ghost appeared at the grave site sobbing and wailing. Unfortunately, he never

called out what his name was. Maybe it was a warning to others not to forget their names or at least to write them down somewhere, even if just on a napkin or the side of a paper bag.

I'm Ho-o-o-o-me
A Wonder in Watseka

Watseka, Illinois is south of Chicago and is reached by taking Highway 57 south, then Route 24 east. It is a small town and you should easily be able to locate the old Roff House. The events are from the later half of the nineteenth century but the story made quite a sensation and was even reported in a book by Dr. E. W. Steffens in 1897.

In 1877, Lurancy Vennum was a seemingly normal fourteen-year-old girl who lived in Watseka, Illinois, with her parents. Mary Roff, on the other hand, was a highly disturbed girl who had been a neighbor of the Vennums and who had died twelve years before in an insane asylum.

One day Lurancy Vennum was suddenly struck with a fit of hysteria for no apparent reason. Her episodes of hysteria became more severe and more frequent. Eventually the teenager began to fall into trances during which she was overcome by the departed spirits of a number of horrifying characters. Finally, one day Lurancy did not completely wake from her trance but told her parents that the spirit of the long-dead Mary Roff was now inhabiting her body. Lurancy had been two years old when Mary Roff had died and therefore could have known little about her.

Having declared herself to be the newly-incarnated spirit of Mary Roff, Lurancy demanded that she be returned 'home' to the Roff residence. At first the Vennums did not allow their daughter to leave, and called their minister and doctor in hopes of bringing Lurancy out of her trance. When this failed Lurancy was taken to where the Roffs lived.

The Roffs were spiritualists and listened to Lurancy's claims of being their deceased daughter inhabiting Lurancy's body. But, if this were so, where was Lurancy? According to Mary Roff's spirit, Lurancy was temporarily in heaven while she was in control of the body.

The Roff's took the girl into their home and were amazed how she knew everyone in the family and how completely at home she was. Not only did she know everyone in the house and every detail of the house itself but she also knew people who had been friends of the Roffs. More than this, she could recount a great many incidents from the life of Mary Roff exactly as they had occurred. Lurancy—now living the life of Mary Roff—did not know any of the Vennum's friends nor even the Vennums themselves. To her, they were complete strangers.

Occasionally she would fall into a mild trance, when she claimed to return to heaven. After a number of weeks, Lurancy would, for short periods, regain control of her former body but soon be returned to heaven to make room for Mary again.

Just as the spirit of Mary Roff had predicted at the outset of her appearance, fourteen weeks later Lurancy Vennum regained full control of her own body. Lurancy emerged from a trance to find herself among strangers in the Roff household. She was then returned to her former home with the Vennums where she rushed into the arms of her natural parents who had been visiting her the entire time. Lurancy did not remember anything of the past weeks. Her description of heaven would certainly have been fascinating to hear if only she had a recollection of being there.

Lurancy's story is extensively documented and can be examined in depth in Doctor Steffen's 1897 book, *The Watseka Wonder*. It's an extremely rare case where a ghost takes physical possession of a body and attempts to resume its former life. It is unlike typical accounts of possession because in them the body is taken control of by a demon or other type of evil spirit, not a ghost as we tend to use the term.

Mary Roff's spirit was that of a normal, though highly disturbed, individual which seemed to have a purpose in mind. It hardly seems a coincidence that she chose to assume control of the body of a female neighbor who was approximately her age when she'd died. This allowed her to step into the body of someone of the right age to be able to resume her old life again with her own family who were close by the home of her host body.

But why did Mary Roff limit her time on earth to a mere fourteen weeks? Could it be that some higher power had granted her a brief reprieve from death to enjoy some last moments with her family while Lurancy was allowed a visit to heaven as recompense for the loss of her time on earth? In all respects what happened in Watseka was a most extraordinary event.

Ghosts of Packers Past

Finally, we have a very odd story from Berwyn, Illinois which is located in the extreme western suburbs of Chicago. You will not find this account in any other book because I believe I am the only person that the witness has told this story to. The sighting occurred at 1941 Ridgeland in an old-fashioned duplex apartment-type building. According to the witness he awoke one night in his bed and found an apparition starting to take shape in his window, appearing from the fire escape outside.

The witness stated that he quite clearly saw first the shoulder, then the rest of the torso, then the head of a husky male form. It appeared to the witness that the muscular apparition was wearing a Green Bay Packers football uniform complete with helmet! It bounded through the window, charged across the room, and disappeared into the wall. No one else was there to see it. When I asked the witness if he was sure he hadn't just imagined this spectral football player or if he might have dreamt it he was adamant about its reality, so adamant that it would be difficult not to believe him. He had seen something! And never saw it again.

What is particularly odd about the sighting is the uniform of the football player. The witness was not a Green Bay Packer fan, so if he had imagined or dreamt the apparition, why would it be wearing a Packer uniform? At least if it'd been wearing a Chicago Bears uniform we could have identified him with the famous Galloping Ghost, Red Grange. But, as it is, we'll have to settle for a rambling Packer instead.

NEAR-GHOSTS

The term 'near-ghosts' harkens back to the term 'near-beer' as used in Cicero, Illinois. Cicero was where Al Capone lived and, in the most extreme of ironies, it is a town that is dry—a place where alcoholic beverages are not allowed. Thus the beer-like beverage called 'near-beer' came into being to satisfy those living in Cicero as a beverage that is like beer but not quite beer.

Pass the Bread, Please

In 1943, a most unusual sighting occurred in Sterling, Illinois. Each night a ghostly hand appeared on one of the inside walls in one of that community's homes. The hand was a ghastly orange color and wrote strange indecipherable messages on the wall. A reporter spent three nights in this house investigating the story which had the whole town terrorized. Whose hand was this and what was the message being written?

'Bread.' That was the message. 'Bread.' The answer to this mystery was unveiled when someone noticed that the orange hand only appeared when a car turned a nearby corner from the right and its headlights splashed on a lighted sign in the window of a grocery store which was directly across the street from the "haunted" house.

The sign in the grocery store advertising bread had blue and red bulbs. When the car lights mingled with those lights a weird orange color was created that was projected from the store window across the street and onto the wall of the "haunted" house's staircase. The result was a fearsome-looking hand and indistinguishable writing.

Unnerving Knockings

A subscriber to the *Sun-Times* in Chicago wrote to one of the columnists complaining of strange noises. According to the letter writer there were hideous howls, piercing whines and unnerving knockings coming from somewhere in the depths of her home. The newspaper sent a reporter to investigate and the mystery was quickly solved. A visit from a local furnace repair company exorcised the annoying spirits. However, it would be interesting to know what might have been incinerated in that furnace over the last ten years. Furnaces have proven to be excellent places for getting rid of troublesome evidence.

Haunted Bars –
Or Was it Just the Last Whiskey?

A story in the *Chicago Sun* from May 1947 described a haunted bar in Leyden, Illinois. Customers heard terrifying whining sounds coming from some hidden place in the building. Many were convinced that it could only be the cries of a ghostly baby. The owner of the bar insisted that the whining was from a missing kitten roaming about the bar. Neither the kitten nor the ghostly baby were located.

EPILOGUE

We've seen a lot of Chicagoland ghosts over these many pages and you've probably noticed their distinct personalities. Some of the spirits are of the gangster-type: Al Capone, James Clark (from the St. Valetine's Day massacre), John Dillinger, and James Lawrence, Dillinger's stand-in at the Biograph shooting.

Another type of Chicagoland spirits are the saintly ghosts: Resurrection Mary, Julia Buccola Petta, and Mary Quinn. They are representative of the strong ethnic background of Chicagoland ghosts and stand in sharp contrast to the ganster spirits.

Another prominent type of ghost in Chicagoland is that of the late nineteenth century-early twentieth century wealthy capitalist/industrialists: William Wrigley, Cyrus McCormick, Louise and Adolph Luetgert, George Stickney, and the great entrepeneur, Richard Warren Sears. The ghosts of these powerful individuals seem to continue to affect the surroundings well after their deaths.

Among the many ghosts we've visited, however, two are of particular importance—not because of their notoriety or fame—but because they are among the least well-known, even obscure. The extremely obscure one occurred on October 26, 1946, and received little news coverage. It concerned a reputedly haunted house in one of the quiet neighborhoods of Chicago. Apparitions were seen and strange noises were heard, yet there was no reason to expect this particular abandoned house to be haunted. The reports of apparitions persisted, however, and soon an investigation was made. The decomposed body of an elderly man was found.

What makes this story so interesting is that the sighting of apparitions at this location could not be attributed to suggestion or mass hallucation because there wasn't any reason for anyone to suspect that the house was haunted.

The other important haunting is at the Red Lion Pub. This is the location where I heard loud stomping sounds coming from the second floor of the restaurant and saw a hurried rush of restaurant staff up the stairs in response to the noises. The staff eventually came back down; but not a single other person left the room on the second floor and not another sound came from above.

It wasn't until several years later that I learned about the ghost who haunts the second floor of the Red Lion Pub, a ghost who makes its appearance at the same time on Sunday afternoons. This would certainly be another hard case for skeptics to explain away. I hadn't been expecting to encounter a ghost and wasn't even aware of the haunted nature of the restaurant, yet I experienced this ghost at the exact time of day when makes its commotion.

So, the next time you hear a strange sound or catch a fleeting glimpse of something inexplicable, don't dismiss it. You may later discover you've encountered a ghost!